NATIONAL GEOGRAPHIC | U.S. HISTORY

AMERICA THROUGH THE LENS
HISTORY NOTEBOOK

Critical Thinking Skills

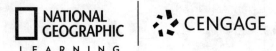

Acknowledgments

Grateful acknowledgment is given to the authors, artists, photographers, museums, publishers, and agents for permission to reprint copyrighted material. Every effort has been made to secure the appropriate permission. If any omissions have been made or if corrections are required, please contact the Publisher.

Credits

Front Cover: (tl) Tetra Images/Getty Images. (tr) Andy Sacks/ Getty Images. (cl) ©Rosalia Torres/Brandon Torres-Weiner. (c) ©Bettmann/Getty Images. (cr) pidjoe/Getty Images. (bl1) Joel Sartore/National Geographic Creative. (bl2) David Hiser/ National Geographic Creative. (bc) Amos Chapple/Getty Images. (br) Library of Congress, LC-DIG-ds-07422.

Back Cover: SpaceX.

"National Geographic", "National Geographic Society" and the Yellow Border Design are registered trademarks of the National Geographic Society ® Marcas Registradas

For product information and technology assistance, contact us at Customer & Sales Support, 888-915-3276

For permission to use material from this text or product, submit all requests online at **www.cengage.com/permissions**

Further permissions questions can be emailed to **permissionrequest@cengage.com**

National Geographic Learning | Cengage
1 N. State Street, Suite 900
Chicago, IL 60602

National Geographic Learning, a Cengage company, is a provider of quality core and supplemental educational materials for the PreK–12, adult education, and ELT markets. Cengage is a leading provider of customized learning solutions with employees residing in nearly 40 different countries and sales in more than 125 countries around the world. Find your local representative at NGL.Cengage.com/RepFinder.

Visit National Geographic Learning online at **NGL.Cengage.com/school**

Visit our corporate website at **www.cengage.com**

ISBN: 978-133-7690-041

Printed in the United States of America

Print number: 03
Print year:2022

Contents

Do you recognize that magazine with the yellow border on newsstands in airports or on shelves in libraries—or maybe even on your coffee table at home? If so, you've probably come to expect from *National Geographic* interesting stories on wide-ranging topics, with great photographs and graphics. But your history text, *America Through the Lens*, has the same goals as that familiar magazine, and we want you to understand the ideas and principles that were so important to its development.

OUR PURPOSE **The National Geographic Society pushes the boundaries of exploration to further our understanding of our planet and empower us all to generate solutions for a healthier and more sustainable future.**

National Geographic Explorer Leslie Dewan is working on a safe alternative to traditional nuclear power.

©National Geographic Creative

Washington, D.C., offices of the National Geographic Society

©Marcie Goodale/National Geographic Learning

NG photographer Jimmy Chin preps for a photo shoot in Yosemite National Park, California.

©Mike Schaefer/National Geographic Creative

We Further Exploration. National Geographic has become one of the largest nonprofit scientific and educational institutions in the world. NatGeo supports hundreds of scientists, archaeologists, marine biologists, divers, climbers, photographers, researchers, teachers, oceanographers, geologists, adventurers, physicists, artists, curators, and writers, all out there "doing their thing." And what they do is not only personally exciting and rewarding to them, it also adds to the scientific and human record.

Today, whether it is at "headquarters" on 17th street in Washington, D.C., or in the field with one of the hundreds of National Geographic Explorers or photographers, the National Geographic Society takes on lots of different activities that support science, exploration, and education. Ever imagine what it would be like to climb Pakistan's treacherous K7 mountain? NatGeo climber and expedition photographer Jimmy Chin has been there. Hanging off the top of one of New York City's skyscrapers to take photos is just a routine day for him. Guillermo de Anda could give you an entirely different perspective—as an underwater archaeologist, he spends much of his time exploring flooded caves on the Yucatan Peninsula. And Sandra Postel, a freshwater conservationist, can tell you what it will take to protect and conserve the world's fresh water in a sustainable way for future generations.

Some of these amazing explorers are featured in your textbook. Check them out—can you see yourself following in their footsteps? There's a world of possibilities for you to discover.

 **The National Geographic Approach**

Terra Cotta Buddha
This 5-foot tall statue was discovered at the site of Hadda in Afghanistan. Artifacts like this one reveal a great deal about the culture that created them.

National Geographic Archaeology Archaeology is an important initiative at National Geographic. Dr. Fred Hiebert, Archaeologist-in-Residence, tackles numerous archaeology projects that take him all over the world. Fred says of archaeology and history:

One of the most precious resources of our world is our human history. We have an archaeological record of humans all over the world and through time. People have been leaving little traces of humanity and identity behind, and this record of stones and bones is an incredible resource for us. But it's different from oceans or trees or animals because it is nonrenewable. Once it's gone, it can never be replaced. That's why the archaeological and historical record is so important—it tells us about human history and the way we have lived on this earth for hundreds of thousands of years. That may hold solutions to how we will live in the future.

The National Geographic Learning Framework As you read your textbook, you'll notice that at the end of every unit there are some activities with the National Geographic Learning Framework label. These activities were created to support the **Attitudes, Skills,** and **Knowledge** that most explorers have. The attributes of the Learning Framework are: **Attitudes**—Curiosity, Responsibility, and Empowerment; **Skills**—Observation; Communication, Collaboration, and Problem-solving; **Knowledge**—The Human Story; Critical Species and Places; Our Changing Planet.

So that's what your history program, *America Through the Lens*, is all about. Our hope is that you will feel connected to the people who came before us, who were part of such critical events in U.S. history. And we know—without you telling us—that you are thinking about your future. Whatever choices you make and whatever direction you follow, we wish you the best for an exciting and rewarding adventure.

NATIONAL GEOGRAPHIC LEARNING SOCIAL STUDIES CREDO

National Geographic Learning wants you to think about the impact of your choices on yourself and others; to think critically and carefully about ideas and actions; to become a lifelong learner and teacher; and to advocate for the greater good as a leader in your community. Your history text follows these guidelines:

1 Our goal is to make the study of history relevant by connecting the physical environment and historical events to your life.

2 We view history as the study of personal identity.

3 We foster the development of empathy, tolerance, and understanding for diverse peoples, cultures, traditions, and ideas.

4 We are determined to empower you to explore your interests and strengths, find your own voices, and speak out on your beliefs.

5 We encourage you to become an active and responsible citizen on local and national levels, and to learn what it means to be a global citizen.

6 We want you to believe in the beauty and endurance of the human record and the need to preserve it.

7 We affirm the critical need to care for the planet and all of its inhabitants.

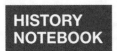

Your *History Notebook* is meant to be a companion to your *America Through the Lens* textbook. In it you'll find worksheets that align to selected lessons in the book. But these are not your typical worksheets—you won't find a single question asking you to recall the date of a battle, the name of a specific president, or the details of an event in history. There is plenty of that in the text itself. Instead, the *History Notebook* asks you to think about issues, form opinions, and provide reasons for those opinions. It is your place to record your thoughts— to think out loud—and to help make sense of what you're reading. Here's what you'll find in the *History Notebook*:

Archaeology and U.S. History

The Archaeology and U.S. History pages in your *America Through the Lens* textbook—and the accompanying *History Notebook* pages—show how archaeology and history work together to interpret history, from more than one side of the story. Be sure to check them out and use them to help you understand how archaeology relates not just to history but also to your own life.

Page 81

Section 1 Student-Centered Learning

Page viii

You may have noticed that the National Geographic name appears on the cover of your textbook. *America Through the Lens* supports the goals and purpose of the National Geographic Society, and some of the National Geographic experts contributed to your text. Read the informal essays in this section of the *History Notebook* to learn more about photography from award-winning National Geographic photographer Ken Garrett; about how museums can be your partners in studying history from National Geographic Vice President for Exhibitions Kathryn Keane; and about bringing history to life through videos from National Geographic's Digital Nomad Robert Reid.

Section 2 Projects for Inquiry-Based Learning

Page xx

The *History Notebook* provides four projects that your teacher might assign to you. These projects range from taking photos and developing a photo essay that describes your life in the United States to working with a few classmates to make a video of a historical re-enactment. You can use the pages in this section of the *History Notebook* to help you plan, conduct, and report out on your project.

Section 3 Lesson Support

Most of the pages in the *History Notebook* are designed to extend your learning from selected lessons in your *America Through the Lens* textbook. (Use the table of contents to locate assigned pages.) You can record your responses to questions on the write-on lines provided, but feel free to continue on your own paper.

U.S. History is an important subject to study. It may sound dusty and boring, but it is a record of how we humans have settled the United States—what we've done well and what we could have done better. And despite the painful conflicts you'll read about, history still captures the most beautiful objects, the most heartfelt moments, and the bravest of actions that humans have to offer. You need to know about them because, believe it or not, you too will have your chance to make a difference, to says words and make decisions that will not only determine how you live your own life but impact those around you. Count on it.

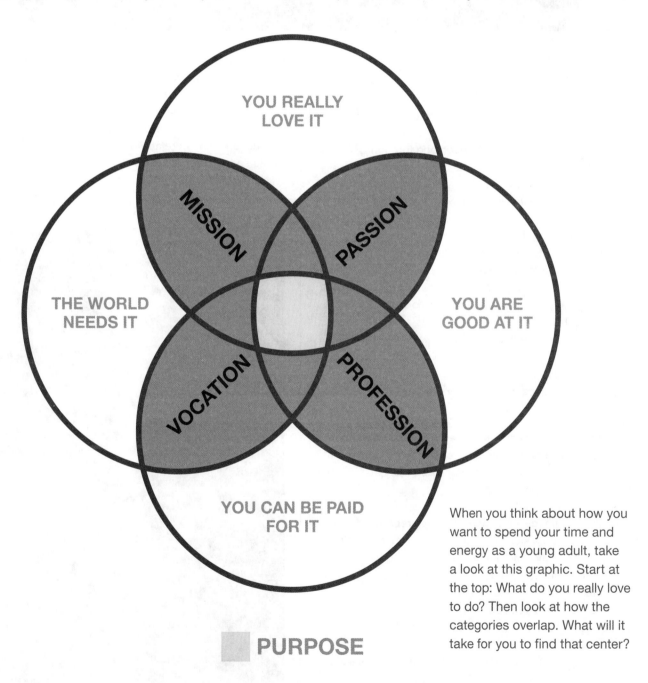

When you think about how you want to spend your time and energy as a young adult, take a look at this graphic. Start at the top: What do you really love to do? Then look at how the categories overlap. What will it take for you to find that center?

National Geography Photography

Ken Garrett is an award-winning photographer who has spent his career capturing compelling images from all over the world, many for the pages of *National Geographic*. Here, he talks about how a would-be photographer can follow in his photographic footprints.

■ By Kenneth Garrett, National Geographic Photographer

Photography as storytelling. For 40 years, I have made photographs for *National Geographic* magazine. Interested in becoming a photographer? Here are some ideas that have guided my approach to photography.

☐ **1. Understand your subject through and through.**
Before you grab your camera and start firing away in order to photograph or illustrate a story, you need to know what you want to share with your audience.

☐ **2. Keep practicing, but complete your education—and have something to say.** As a high school student, I was fortunate enough to be able to ask the National Geographic Director of Photography, Bob Gilka, what his thoughts were on studying to be a photographer. He was very clear and concise, and he said, "Go to a liberal arts college and get a good education, so that when you take pictures you will have something to say." I have held this advice close to my heart throughout my career—always working to make sure that my photographs have something to say.

My work has led me to photograph from fossil finds more than 4 million years old as part of a story on human evolution to the ongoing struggle for civil rights in America today. I'm always looking for an important story that can be told in a series of photographs.

☐ **3. Craft each image with intent, and be prepared.**
I was working on a story in Guatemala on remote imaging of Maya cities. My editor knew there was going to be a planetary alignment of Venus, Jupiter, and Mars, directly over a temple in Tikal, and that it would not happen again for 200 years. Of course he wanted me to get a photograph of it. I brought a portable spotlight to "paint" the temple with light and made a wonderful photo with the planets aligned over the temple. This is what I call making your own luck—being prepared and ready for what's about to happen.

Another example of preparation: I was in Mexico photographing a story on the Olmec civilization, and learned about a festival where the ancient rain god was invoked in a dance ceremony. One small boy was being prepared to be the jaguar in the dance. His body was smeared with mud, and they were applying the spots of the jaguar with an old soda bottle. The proud look of the boy standing still for his decoration made this photo (shown below) the one we published, rather than the actual dancing in the streets.

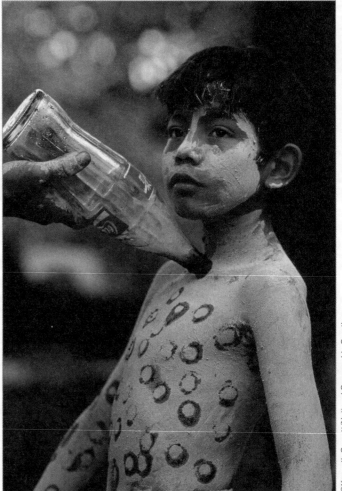

4. Look over each subject very carefully to figure out lighting and how to make it "pop." If my subject is an artifact in a museum, I study it with a flashlight until I find an angle where it "speaks to me." Then I begin to create a lighting setup to bring out the personality that I identified with the flashlight. Sometimes I even make the photo by "painting" the object with the light from the flashlight. Photographs are made up of light, so lighting the subject, whether it is an object, a landscape, or an architectural feature, is most important. The image must "pop" and readers must say "wow," or they won't stop to learn—there is simply too much visual competition out there.

5. Be passionate about your work, and learn everything you can about your specialty. I have a passion for the study of culture, and I have been very lucky to spend my career chasing state-of-the-art information on ancient civilizations throughout the world. It is imperative to have a strong passion for your specialty if you want to be successful in photography. The more you know about the subject and the scientists doing the work, the better able you are to communicate important new discoveries to the readers.

6. Get to know your subject. Get to know the key scientists or historians in the field and find out what they are doing. Learn about their field research in case you can visit them in the field at some point in the future. Most importantly, know when they have a breakthrough in scientific knowledge that will interest the media editors. I have lectured on the topic "What happens if a tree falls?" It is all about being there to photograph the moment of discovery and then to publish it in the popular media for everyone to see. Without media coverage, many great discoveries lie silent on shelves in storerooms around the world.

Regardless of the field you feel passionate about, the process is the same. Know the subject. Know the people. Know how to be in the right place at the right time. One of my good friends is an underwater photographer, and aside from the technology of underwater photography, his specialty is the biology of the sea creatures he wishes to document: their habits, their locations, their feeding patterns. Choose your passion and learn everything you can about the subject.

7. Be adaptable, but don't be afraid to develop your own vision. I was trained to be a generalist, flexible, able to adapt to any situation. I was identified as the photographer to send if there was nothing to photograph, because I'd *find* something to photograph. In today's world, I still believe it is important to be adaptable, but the market is often looking for

photographers with a unique specialty, a unique look—a way of seeing that translates into your own unique style.

8. Develop a portfolio of your photographs. So how do you get started in a photography career? The traditional way is to work for your school newspaper, study journalism, and then get a starter job making photographs for your local newspaper. Once you have built a portfolio, you can start approaching major national publications. Many young photographers choose to pursue assignments in war zones to see if they can make a name for themselves—a dangerous method not suited to all personalities. Today, with Instagram, Facebook, and other platforms, you can have your photos "out there" for all to see as soon as you shoot them.

9. Build relationships with photo editors. They are the ones who hire photographers. Having a passion and a vision and a Facebook account will not get you jobs unless you establish relationships within the photo community. I spent a great deal of time showing my portfolio to major publications. I lugged a Kodak Carousel projector and slide tray from office to office, often with a proposal in hand for a story idea suited to their publication, hoping they would like what they saw enough to give me a chance at shooting a story.

10. Follow the new technology in photography. Today's cameras have eliminated much of the technical difficulty of capturing an image. Auto focus. Auto Exposure. Auto White Balance. Auto ISO adjustment. Automatic Flash. What is left to do? Many of the basic skills I learned are no longer necessary: Choosing a film type. Choosing the developer. Choosing the paper to print on.

With this new technology comes exciting new opportunities to "push the envelope"—for example, to shoot in virtual darkness, shoot remotely, shoot from a drone, shoot through a hole less than one inch in diameter, or shoot underwater from a remotely operated submersible. These new skills are no less complicated than the analog processes of old—always changing, sometimes for the better, sometimes just for the sake of change. Constantly following the new technology is a requirement of today's photography business.

11. Be prepared for the lifestyle of a photographer. It is exciting, but not for everyone. You have to be prepared to be away from home for weeks or months at a time, living with your subject until just the right situation presents itself: until a rapport is established that allows you special access to an event, until a discovery is made, or until a polar bear walks up to your camera!

Kathryn Keane has one of the best jobs in the whole world. As Vice President, Exhibitions, at the National Geographic Museum in Washington, D.C., Kathryn is responsible for bringing to the American public a wide range of displays that include an amazing collection of golden Peruvian artifacts, an interactive exhibit on freshwater "monsterfish" from across the globe, and a photography exhibit of the best National Geographic photos on Instagram. She's an expert on museums—take advantage of her ideas for your next museum visit!

■ By Kathryn Keane, Vice President, Exhibitions, National Geographic Society

When I want to take a trip into the past, to actually immerse myself in history, I go to a museum. Museums are like time machines. They are the keepers of our shared and collective history. They contain collections of things. Anthropologists categorize these human-made objects as **material culture**. Museums were created to keep track of the most special examples of material culture. Paintings, sculpture, pottery, jewelry, clothing, furniture, cars, toys, weapons, tools, fishing lures—just about anything that humans make is a remarkable historic record of the way we live. So when anthropologists call the Smithsonian "the nation's attic," they aren't wrong. It is just the coolest attic you have ever been in and contains the treasures of our history.

Some of those treasures are featured in the "Curating History" lessons in this program. Each of these lessons features objects drawn from the collection of an important museum in the United States—and each provides a window to a time period in our nation's history.

But what do we learn from this stuff? Why are some things in a museum and others are not?

Generally, museums look for the best artifacts for their collections, the ones that helped to define a people or culture. Egyptian sarcophagi, Peruvian face pots, African ceremonial masks, Venetian glass, Native American pottery, or Cycladic figurines from the Greek islands are all examples of artifacts that help us better understand those who made them. People from thousands of miles away and hundreds of years ago feel more familiar when you observe that, like us, they ate on plates and drank from cups, had rugs on their floors, keys for their doors,

and rocked their babies to sleep in wooden cradles. Material culture is the study of what humans make—but also what makes us human. There is no better way to see this than in a museum.

Check out these tips for your next museum visit. Planning ahead makes all the difference between a confusing or unsatisfying visit, and one that can actually change your perspective on your country.

1. **Plan ahead.** Before you visit, do your homework about the history of the museum and its collection. Most museums have great websites, and many even have their entire collections online. Take some time to research the collection and the must-see artifacts and works of art so you'll know what to look for. The more you know before you arrive, the better prepared you will be to get the most out of the experience.

2. **Get a friend to go, and check in once you get there.** Museums are supposed to be shared experiences. While I've spent many days lost in museums by myself over the years, the best experiences were with family, classmates, or friends. Once you arrive, check in with the information desk. Get a map and ask questions about the highlights of the collection and any special exhibitions or events going on.

3. **Experience the museum from the beginning to the end.** There are usually lots of interesting stories that are told in a museum—experiencing an exhibition is a bit like walking through the pages of a good book. While it is possible to skip forward in the experience, it's best to start from the beginning and follow the

story the way it is designed to be viewed. Sometimes exhibits are immersive lessons in history. Sometimes they are installations that express an artist's point of view. In either case, the more you know ahead of time, the better your experience will be.

4. **Read, listen, and learn.** Labels, maps, timelines, videos, audio tours, and other instructional materials will give you all the information you need about what you see in the museum. Be sure to read the introduction panels that give the big picture for each gallery. Individual labels provide information about each specific artifact or work of art.

Museum educators use maps, videos, and timelines to tell the rest of the story. This extra information provides important "context" for the art and the artifacts in the museum. Audio tours, if available, are usually narrated by a curator, or expert, and are almost like getting a private tour. This is especially helpful if you are in a country where the labels and other content are not in your native language.

Use a form similar to the one on the next page to help you analyze an artifact and record your reactions to it.

The National Geographic Museum hosted an exhibition entitled "The Greeks: Agamemnon to Alexander the Great" in 2016. This exhibition gathered more than 500 artifacts, many of which had never traveled outside of Greece.

©Marcie Goodale/National Geographic Learning

5. **Dos and Don'ts** Follow these tips to make sure that everyone has a good museum experience. Feel free to talk to your friends, family, or teachers about what you are seeing, but remember that the people around you are having their own experiences. Keeping your voice down and leaving your phone in your pocket (and turned off) is polite and respectful. Don't touch artifacts or lean on cases. Don't take pictures unless it is expressly allowed, and make sure you are careful around fragile or delicate objects.

6. **Use your imagination.** Think about the things you are seeing and what they mean. Imagine what it was like to live a long time ago or in a faraway place—or even in the mind of a creative artist. Albert Einstein famously said, "Logic will get you from A to B. Imagination will take you everywhere." Imagine a future museum. What will students 100 years from now be learning about our society in a museum?

7. **After your visit** If you picked up a brochure about the museum, it may have information about how you can learn more. Take advantage of the resources available to you, and remember that a museum's website is often full of additional content on the collections and the special exhibitions. Encourage your family to think about joining the museum—members get special privileges throughout the year and can come back as often as they like with no additional fee.

Enjoy the museums in your hometown or extended community. As you travel, don't forget to check out the museums in the places you visit!

HISTORY NOTEBOOK | Artifact Analysis Form

NATIONAL GEOGRAPHIC
L E A R N I N G

Museum: _____

Location: _____

ARTIFACT	NOTES
What is this object?	
What is the object made from?	
What technology might have been required to make it?	
Describe the shape, color, and size of the object.	
How might the object have been used? What clues led you to that conclusion?	
What time period does it date from?	
What people or culture might have produced it?	
What can you infer about the lives of the people who made or used this object?	

NatGeo's Digital Nomad Takes On U.S. History

Robert Reid leads a life some of us might very well envy—who *wouldn't* want to hike in Ethiopia? Or float on some of the most exotic rivers in the world? Or—as Robert did to make the videos for this U.S. History program—play in a jazz band in New Orleans? Here, Robert explains his approach to connecting the study of history to world travel, and the questions that make him most curious.

■ By Robert Reid, National Geographic's Digital Nomad

©Robert Reid/National Geographic Creative

Every time I travel to a place as National Geographic's Digital Nomad, my first questions are the same: what happened there, what books and movies talk about it, and how can I add an angle to the ongoing story, something that adds to the existing conversation? In short, my focus is looking backward to look forward. I do that by putting history into travel. It's fun and informative. Working on this *America Through the Lens* textbook is the same, but in reverse direction—in trying to show how history is alive and accessible, I'm putting it through the filter of travel.

Digital nomad Robert Reid interviews a Rosie-the-Riveter re-enactor on the job.

©Robert Reid/National Geographic Creative

For each of the videos that accompany *America Through the Lens*, we talk with local experts—including those impersonating Rosie the Riveter, overseeing Motown records, and building old Model Ts—and go up close and personal. The goal is to bring a question or two that, I hope, you'll be curious about: Why is the Statue of Liberty the greatest gift of all time? Where did jazz come from? What's a hippie? Then I use travel to answer those questions.

And in some cases, I weld rivets to do so. (Watch the videos—you'll see.)

Perhaps my favorite story about developing the *Reid on the Road* video series was visiting Angel Island in San Francisco Bay. I lived in the city several years ago,

and had never made it there, nor did I realize that it was, in effect, the Ellis Island of the West. Going there, I interviewed a Chinese American whose father entered the country through Angel Island, and heard the stories of how immigrants entering the country from the west didn't exactly get the same reception as those entering through New York. I'll not forget it.

The goal, again, is to make a difference in your understanding of this country—and to show how history isn't relegated to the past, but is indeed alive. It moves, it changes. And how we use it is how we go through life. This may sound serious, but it's the first step in our personal chase of understanding. Which means that, like travel itself, it's about as much fun as you can have.

PROJECTS FOR INQUIRY-BASED LEARNING
Through the Lens Project

Studying the history of our country helps each of us understand what it means to be American and how our American identity is shaped by where we live in the United States. Through text, visuals, and video you've explored the elements that create the American experience. Now it's time to express your own experience.

One way to explore and express our unique American identities is through photography. When you look through the camera lens, you see things from a different perspective. Your focus is drawn to the object, person, or place that tells a story. Welcome to the "Through the Lens" photo essay project. This is your opportunity to look through the lens and document your America through a collection of photos created by you—it's your American experience.

Here is what to do:

1. Document "your America" by creating a collection of photos that captures what your life in this country is like. Choose a city to photograph that is important to you. It could be your small rural town or the big city you live in, a city that you have visited, or any location that has meaning to you and is part of "your America."

2. Use the camera on your cell phone (or a regular camera) to take photos in your chosen location. You will submit 4 to 5 photos total. You will photograph places that represent your community in some way, like your school, the local library, a statue of the town's founder, maybe a lake or park. You will also photograph places that are particularly special to you, such as your backyard, the baseball field or dance studio where you spend a lot of time, the bus or train station you use to get around, or your favorite restaurant or coffee shop.

3. Record the 4 to 5 locations you plan to photograph in your Photographer's Log (included with the project). Be sure to identify the location specifically.

4. Follow these guidelines as you prepare and take your photographs:

   - Be sure you are accompanied by an adult as you take your photos.

   - Be sure your camera/cell phone is fully charged before setting out.

   - Practice with your camera ahead of time.

   - Set aside plenty of time to take your photos so you're not rushed.

   - Check your camera settings to be sure you are taking photos that are the highest-resolution (largest file size) as possible.

   - Choose a relatively clear day, but it doesn't have to be sunny. In fact, many photographers feel that photos taken in the morning or evening, or in cloudy conditions turn out best.

   - Your photos should not feature people unless they are at a distance. No selfies!

   - Take your Photographer's Log and a pen with you. Record the location of each photo and take notes on why you chose your locations so you can write photo captions later.

   - Take multiple photos at each location from different angles and perspectives, but remember that you will only submit one photo from each location. Once you have finished shooting at a location, you can review your photos, deleting those you don't plan to use. Or you can move on to the next location and leave the photo selection process for when you get back home. It's always better to have many photos to choose from than too few.

HISTORY NOTEBOOK | **PROJECTS FOR INQUIRY-BASED LEARNING**
Through the Lens Project

5. When you are done taking your photos, select one photo from each of your locations. Then write a caption for the photos in your Photographer's Log. Your captions should provide a short description of each place you chose to photograph and explain a little bit about what the photo shows and why you chose to include it in your collection.

6. Complete the "About the Photographer" part of your log to share a little information about you. Include where you live, your interests, and the school you attend.

7. Submit your photos and Photographer's Log to present to the class.

Think About Your America Answer the questions below to get you thinking about the story you want your photo essay to tell about your America.

1. What makes this place "home" for you?

_____

_____

_____

_____

2. What do you love best about where you live? What would you change?

_____

_____

_____

_____

3. What story do you want to tell about where you live?

_____

_____

_____

_____

_____

_____

_____

_____

_____

HISTORY NOTEBOOK | THROUGH THE LENS PROJECT
Photographer's Log

NATIONAL GEOGRAPHIC
L E A R N I N G

As you take your photos, you'll want to create a Photographer's Log that includes a short biography about you, your photos, and captions for each photo. Review the sample Photographer's Log on the next two pages.

Name: Tanya Janik

About the Photographer I'm a 16-year-old teenager living in Libertyville, Illinois, which is about 40 miles north of Chicago. I go to Libertyville High School. I live with my parents and my younger brother. I like to play soccer and I get to do a lot of traveling because of that. I also like photography. I just got a drone, so I'm learning how to take photographs with that.

Photo 1: My House

This is a photograph of my house in Libertyville, Illinois. I have lived here since I was five years old, with my parents, my younger brother, and two dogs. Home represents many things to me—it represents family, a safe and secure base, and community. Even though I like to go out with my friends, I spend so much of my time here in this house, and I kind of like that it represents the fact that Libertyville is an old community. Our house is almost 100 years old, as are many of the other homes in my neighborhood. In this photo, you can see that we've decorated it for Halloween. My dad likes to go all-out with the decorations, and if you travel down my street, you'll see that other people like to do so as well.

Photo 2: Our Bike Path (the DesPlains River Trail)

I spend a lot of time on this path, walking to and from school, running when I am in training for soccer season, walking our dogs, and biking around. I enjoy riding my bike and by sticking to the bike path, I avoid the busier streets in my town. I think we're lucky to have such a nice, wooded path. Even better is that it runs right behind my house.

THROUGH THE LENS PROJECT
Photographer's Log

Photo 3: Homecoming Parade

I took this photo from a long-distance perspective because I wanted to show more of where I live and the community I live in. Every fall, there is a community parade that takes place when the high school celebrates Homecoming. It's not a long parade, but local groups, teams, and organizations get to be part of it, including the high school marching band. I have marched in it many times as part of my soccer team. Almost everyone in the town comes out to cheer on the parade, and kids gather up the candy the marchers throw. This photo shows some of our downtown area up the hill.

© National Geographic Learning

Photo 4: The Soccer Field

Aside from my house, and school, the soccer field is where I spend a lot of my time. This photograph shows my brother's middle school team, in white uniforms, lined up before a game. When I'm not playing soccer, I'm usually watching it and taking photos of the game. It's good practice if I want to be a sports photographer. Again, taken from a long distance, you can see the well-kept field and the landscape of our town.

© National Geographic Learning

Name _____

Now it's time to prepare your photo log. Have you taken your photos yet? Which ones are you going to use? Review your photographs and select the ones that best tell your American story. Don't forget to write a short paragraph that tells a bit about you.

About the Photographer: _____

_____

_____

_____

_____

_____

_____

_____

_____

Photo 1: _____ (location)

_____

_____

_____

_____

_____

_____

_____

_____

_____

_____

_____

Attach your photo

Name _____

Photo 2: _____ (location)

_____

_____

_____

_____

_____

_____

_____

_____

_____

_____

_____

Attach your photo

Photo 3: _____ (location)

_____

_____

_____

_____

_____

_____

_____

_____

_____

_____

_____

Attach your photo

Name _____

Photo 4: _____ (location)

_____
_____
_____
_____
_____
_____
_____
_____
_____
_____
_____
_____
_____

Attach your photo

Photo 5: _____ (location)

_____
_____
_____
_____
_____
_____
_____
_____
_____
_____
_____
_____
_____

Attach your photo

Name _____

Now you've completed your photographer's log, including your collection of photos and the captions to go with it. It's time to present your photo essay documenting your America. Use the questions below to help with your presentation and to review what you've learned.

1. What story does your photo essay tell?

_____

_____

_____

_____

2. Why did you select the photos you selected? You might want to share your reason for each photograph.

_____

_____

_____

_____

_____

_____

_____

_____

3. What did you like best about creating your photo essay?

_____

_____

_____

_____

4. If you were to do a longer photo essay with more visuals, what would you include? How would those photos add to or change your story?

_____

_____

_____

_____

5. How did "looking through the lens" give you a different perspective of your America?

_____

_____

_____

HISTORY NOTEBOOK
PROJECTS FOR INQUIRY-BASED LEARNING
The Generations Oral History Project

You've been reading about history, but there are other ways to learn about past events. When you and your friends get together, you talk and tell stories about your day, your family, things you like to do, and experiences you've had. That verbal interaction is a lot different than reading third-hand about your friend's experience in basketball practice.

An oral history provides a personal account of an event from someone who has firsthand knowledge of it. For this project, you will create your own oral history by interviewing people about their experience with a specific event. Learn about oral history—what it is, why it matters, and how to create one—from National Geographic Explorer Caroline Gerdes as she guides you through the process.

My Oral History Project

By Caroline Gerdes, oral historian and National Geographic Explorer

©Robert Giglio/National Geographic Learning

Can you imagine going to the first high school football game of the season, sleeping at a friend's house, and waking up to a Category 5 hurricane barreling toward your family, friends, school, grocery store, favorite hangout—everything? Well, that's what happened to me.

When I was 15 years old (in 2005), Hurricane Katrina in New Orleans, Louisiana, crashed my sophomore year of high school. My home was without power for weeks, and I was out of school for about two months. My friends were scattered as refugees throughout the South, actually throughout the entire United States. A few of them I never saw again. And my 85-year-old grandmother lost everything she owned as floodwaters washed above ceiling-level in her home.

In the months following Hurricane Katrina, as we sorted through the wreckage at my grandmother's house, I learned valuable lessons about what can be salvaged, what we remember about a significant time, and the temporary existence of most objects. I learned that some things are worth rebuilding and remembering. This passion for documenting modern history and important moments stayed with me into adulthood and fueled my interest in **oral history**, which is collecting historical

information by recording interviews with people who experienced past events.

Your stories are already being written and are well worth preserving, just like mine were when I was about your age. Our stories may be different, but that's the interesting thing about oral history. Think of the stories you see unfolding on broadcast news or the articles you read online or in the paper. These stories are the first drafts of history. Your experience reading about them and the things you feel when reacting to everyday news, politics, and events could be recorded as oral history.

In my experience as an oral historian, oral history provides firsthand accounts of historical events and everyday experiences, while people who have living memory of these moments are still able to share their stories. These people, or narrators, are interviewed about their memories as part of an oral history collection or archive. There are many types of oral history projects. Some record many different age groups after a recent news event, like the September 11 terrorist attacks or Hurricane Katrina. Some ask for people from a certain location or group to come forward and share experiences. Other oral history projects target an age

Damage and destruction to New Orleans' Ninth Ward during Hurricane Katrina took years to repair.

group to record stories of times gone by. And some projects focus on people who were present at a historic event before firsthand stories are lost to time. All of these projects have the common thread of preserving stories of cant events through the experiences of everyday people.

In 2012, when I was 22 years old, I received a National Geographic Young Explorers Grant to conduct an oral history project in my own backyard. In the years after Hurricane Katrina, the Ninth Ward in New Orleans never regained its pre-Katrina population. Landmarks with historic significance, like churches and school campuses, sat vacant. They were at risk of being demolished or further altered by another storm or event. The Ninth Ward's original residents from its days as a turn-of-the-century immigrant borough were elderly and passing away. There was an urgency to document the Ninth Ward's story while the landmarks stood and some of its oldest residents were still living. With support from National Geographic, I was able to record these stories by interviewing about 50 people who called the Ninth

Ward home. This project also had personal significance because my dad and his parents—my grandparents—grew up in the Ninth Ward.

I recorded stories about the Ninth Ward's evolution throughout the 20th century from its immigrant origins to the Depression to the Civil Rights movement. The Ninth Ward was actually ground zero for school desegregation in New Orleans. In November 1960, Ruby Bridges desegregated William Frantz Elementary School in the Ninth Ward on the same day three brave little girls desegregated McDonogh 19, also in the Ninth Ward. These girls were known as the McDonogh Three, and one of the women in the group, Leona Tate, spoke to me about her historic experience more than 50 years later. I also documented stories from historic hurricanes spanning from the 1940s through Hurricane Katrina. But some of my favorite memories to record were about everyday life and traditions in the community.

Having these voices on record is important not just for neighborhood history, but also to show what life was like at a specific time and place in Louisiana, and even America. It's amazing how much can be learned from just one community, and it's more amazing how much can be learned from one family member. By interviewing my grandmother, I had a greater understanding of her life and her identity, which is something that is fascinating for future generations to discover.

My grandmother was the first person I interviewed for my oral history project. I feel fortunate that I spoke with her when I did in 2012. In 2014, she passed away. Just as the Ninth Ward was forever altered, so was the group of people I interviewed. In the years after my project, I lost other narrators, making me so glad I documented the community when I did. It feels significant that I was able to meet so many wonderful people and record their stories at what would prove to be the end of their lives. Oral history, it seems, can be a service.

My National Geographic project taught me the significance of preserving memory. And some of the most personal and important parts of my work can be replicated at home or school. We can all take a moment to record our families, our friends, and our homes. Things are constantly changing, and we are the narrators in our own stories.

 **THE GENERATIONS ORAL HISTORY PROJECT**
Plan Your Project

Before you can even begin your project, you need to plan it. Where do you start? What do you need? What do you hope to accomplish with your project? These are just some of the things to think about and decide before you start. Follow the steps below to plan your project.

A. Think About Oral History Take a moment to think about what you have learned so far about oral history and answer the questions below.

1. What does an oral history do?

_____

_____

2. What do you get from oral stories that you don't get from written stories?

_____

_____

_____

B. Plan Your Topic and Set a Purpose As you read about Caroline Gerdes' oral history project, did it spark ideas for you? Think about a true-life story you might want to tell, an experience in your school or community that you've wondered about, or a news broadcast or article about an event that interests you. If needed, take a little time to conduct online research.

3. What is the subject of your oral history project? What stories are you looking to record?

_____

_____

_____

4. What is the goal of your project? What do you want to learn?

_____

_____

_____

C. Identify Your Interviewees You will need to identify three people to interview for your oral history. These could be people from your family, in your neighborhood, or at school. Once you decide whom you will interview, make sure you get permission to interview each person.

5. Whom will you interview? A certain age group? People from a certain neighborhood? A family member?

_____

_____

_____

_____

_____

THE GENERATIONS ORAL HISTORY PROJECT
Plan Your Project

D. What You'll Need You probably already have everything you need to conduct an oral history project in your pocket.

Recording: You can use a voice recorder or the recorder on your smartphone, laptop, or other device.

Photos: Don't forget to take a picture of your narrator, or with your narrator. You can use a camera or your smartphone.

Videos: Not all oral history projects require video. But you could use your smartphone, laptop, or a video camera to capture footage if you choose to.

Notebook and Pen: Technology is great, but sometimes it fails. In addition to checking your equipment throughout the interview, be sure to take notes. This will help you listen and adapt your questions throughout the interview.

Save Your Work: If you can, store your interview in the same place you store music on your computer. Be sure to type up your interview in order to save a transcript.

If you choose to record your interviews on video, here are some helpful tips on how to set up your camera.

Getting the shot: Try not to have your oral history narrator look directly at the camera. Instead, think about the shot in lines of thirds. (See example at right.) This is not a true profile angle—both of the person's cheeks should be in the shot. The camera is just almost to the side of the narrator. Refer to the photo and note how her gaze is toward the side of the frame with open space. Also, notice that there is not a lot of room above her head.

Lighting: Try to avoid glare and strange shadows. Sitting near a window with light or open shades is best. Natural light usually looks better.

Pay attention to your sound: If you can, listen to the sound via headphones while you set up to avoid feedback. Try recording inside but make sure to avoid noisy fans and humming appliances like fish tanks and refrigerators.

©FangXiaNuo/Getty Images

Make a list of materials you need to bring with you for conducting your interviews.

_____

_____

_____

_____

_____

_____

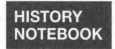

THE GENERATIONS ORAL HISTORY PROJECT

HISTORY NOTEBOOK

The Interview—Draft Your Questions

At this point in your project, you should have your subject decided, your purpose determined, and your interviewees identified, as well as all the tools you need to start interviewing. But what about the questions? Read on to prepare for the interview process.

A. What Questions Should I Ask? Now you're ready to start writing your interview questions. Review Caroline Gerdes' tips below before you write your final questions.

First, ask all of your narrators to first give their name (spelled aloud), date of interview, and relation to what you are discussing.

For example, my Ninth Ward oral history narrator said, "My name is John Smith. J-O-H-N S-M-I-T-H. I lived at 123 Main Street from 1940 to 1970 in the Ninth Ward."

This is a verbal signature. In addition to being a good warm-up, the verbal signature and information is helpful when creating works from audio or video footage later.

Next, start out with broad questions like, "What drew you to contribute to this project?" Tailor your questions beforehand based on time period, geographic location, and personal experience.

There is one question at the end of every oral history interview, or any interview for that matter, that is often the most important. Make sure to always ask the narrator, "Is there anything else you would like to add?" As generic as this may sound, I've gotten some of the best answers with this as my final question.

B. Example Interview Questions Let's pretend you are doing an oral history project about how your school has changed over the past 25 years. Here are some questions you could ask your principal. Before you begin, have your principal spell his/her name aloud and provide how many years he/she has been working at your school.

1. **What inspired you to get into education?** Asking people what drew them to the subject you are discussing is a good way to start an interview.

2. **What was your first day at this school like?** Note how this question gets more specific.

3. **What was your experience like when the big storm flooded campus in 1999?** We want the principal to talk about an important event or action in the school's history. We are also avoiding questions that could have yes or no answers.

4. **What have the students taught you?** This will cause your principal to recall many moments throughout his/her career, instead of focusing on one date.

5. **What do you see for the future of the school?** While oral history focuses on the past, it's always interesting to ask what someone with experience thinks about the future of the subject you are discussing.

6. **Is there anything else you would like to add?** Don't forget this important question!

C. Write Your Interview Questions Write at least five questions you will ask during your interviews below.

1. _____

2. _____

3. _____

4. _____

5. _____

 **THE GENERATIONS ORAL HISTORY PROJECT**
The Interview—During and After

Now you have your interview questions ready, but before you conduct your interview, think about how you will get answers and what you will do with the information you gathered during your interviews. Read the tips below for how to get answers to your questions and how to record your interview notes.

A. Getting Answers

Listen Closely: Your narrator may answer a question before you get to it on your list of questions. So it is important that you listen to answers and show respect by not asking a question that has already been answered. You may have to adapt questions as you go.

Finding the Right Words: If a narrator needs a minute to find the right words, that is ok. Pauses happen in interviews, and sometimes interrupting a silence can throw your narrator off track. Interruptions, *mm-hmms,* and audible responses from an interviewer can throw the narrator off. This can be bad for recorded audio too.

B. Recording Tips

Transcribing and Indexing: After the interview, an oral historian's job is not done. Perhaps the most tedious part of an interview is transcribing, or typing the entire interview word for word. But there is a shortcut that professionals use—indexing. An oral historian may index an interview by typing up every question asked, with a time stamp, or the time in the audio at which the question was asked, next to it. The oral historian will then only type important answers and quotes, with time stamps included. So an indexed interview is not typed word for word. Only an oral historian's favorite parts and significant findings are typed.

Here is an example of what a transcribed oral history question vs. an indexed oral history question would look like:

Transcribed:

What inspired you to get into education?

Well, when I was in fifth grade, or was it sixth grade? I can't remember. I had this fabulous teacher. What was her name? Mrs. Thomas? No, Ms. Tompkins! Well, anyway. I was diagnosed with dyslexia in the sixth grade because I had a great teacher, Ms. Tompkins, who noticed and put in the extra time to help me. She was so great and such a wonderful teacher. That really inspired me. I never forgot her, and here I am—a principal. But, yeah, Ms. Tompkins. She was a great lady.

Indexed:

What inspired you to get into education? [00:01:30]

[00:02:10] I was diagnosed with dyslexia in the sixth grade because I had a great teacher, Ms. Tompkins, who noticed and put in the extra time to help me. She was so great and such a wonderful teacher. That really inspired me. I never forgot her, and here I am — a principal. [00:02:35]

THE GENERATIONS ORAL HISTORY PROJECT
Conduct Your Oral History

Now it's time for you to do your own oral history. This is when all the planning and drafting you did will help you conduct your oral history. Record your interviews, and take notes in your notebook or use the space below. After your interviews are complete, take time to index your interviews in your notebook.

_____

_____

_____

_____

_____

_____

_____

_____

_____

_____

_____

_____

_____

_____

_____

_____

_____

_____

_____

_____

_____

_____

_____

HISTORY NOTEBOOK | **THE GENERATIONS ORAL HISTORY PROJECT**
Write Your Oral History

Congratulations! Your interviews are complete, and you've indexed your notes. Now you can put all the information together to finalize your project. Take time to review your notes and decide what information to use. Look for the key ideas, interesting quotes, and specific details. Then write your oral history below.

_____

_____

_____

_____

_____

_____

_____

_____

_____

_____

_____

_____

_____

_____

_____

_____

_____

_____

_____

_____

_____

_____

1. What did you learn from doing your oral history project?

_____

_____

2. What did you enjoy most about this project? Explain your answer.

_____

_____

 **PROJECTS FOR INQUIRY-BASED LEARNING**

The Story of a Decade

Many events throughout U.S. history have shaped the American identity. By studying our past, we can better understand who we are as a nation today. For this project, you will explore the American experience from 1900 to 2020 by digging in-depth into a narrow time period of a decade. Focusing on American history, culture, daily life, literature, art, music, and economics in the decade, you will show how events and ideas have changed throughout that time period as well as across decades. Use these pages in your History Notebook to research and record information about the decade you are investigating.

DIRECTIONS AND REQUIREMENTS: For this project, you will work in a small group of two or three. Each group will be assigned (or choose) a decade to research, starting at 1900. As a group, you will present to the class your decade's story to provide an overall idea of what it would be like to live at that time.

A. Project Steps Take a look at the steps below before you get started.

1. Get into your group. Decide as a group how you will divide up each aspect of the era to research.

2. Each group will research the following aspects for their decade: history, culture, daily life, literature, art, music, and economics—and anything else that appeals to you. Look for specific themes.

3. Use any additional information you think people would find interesting or would want to know about a specific time period. This is also the opportunity to use your imagination—include speeches, quotes, photographs, illustrations, diagrams, video clips, and even song lyrics to tell the story of that decade.

4. Decide as a group how you will present your finished project. Be as creative as you like. Remember, this is meant to be fun.

B. Project Requirements The requirements listed below will help give you a general framework for the project.

1. The group provides thorough information about the assigned decade.

2. At least three different credible resources are used for research.

3. All group members participate in the research and creation of the project, including the final presentation. Be sure to identify who was responsible for which piece.

4. Final presentation must be complete. Again, use your imagination—find creative ways to present your decade's story. While visuals are not mandatory, they are highly recommended.

C. Presentation Format Some ideas for your final presentation might include:

- Poster display, student web site, or original video
- Debate about the "best" or "worst" or "most exciting" decade
- Memoir from the perspective of a person living in that decade

- Traditional written report
- Original song, poem, or skit
- Media presentation
- Annotated and/or illustrated time line

More than anything, this project is meant to be not only creative and engaging but also a way for you to practice your research, presentation, and multimedia skills. Have fun!

THE STORY OF A DECADE
Research and Data

By now your group has an assigned decade. Did you decide as a group what your final format for your presentation will be? Make sure you have an idea so as you research, you can start collecting images or other items that you'll need for the presentation. Keep in mind that as you research, you might come up with other ideas of how to present your decade. Be open to the possibilities.

Our group decade is _____.

Our final presentation format is _____.

Some things I am looking for are _____.

Now you are ready to start your research and record your data. Use the questions and prompts below as you research. Then use the spaces below to record your notes.

A. History

1. What key events took place during this time period?

_____

_____

_____

_____

_____

_____

_____

_____

2. Who were some of the key historical figures at this time?

_____

_____

_____

_____

_____

_____

_____

_____

_____

HISTORY NOTEBOOK THE STORY OF A DECADE
Research and Data

You've gone through one aspect of your decade. What did you find? Now might be a good time to check in with your group, share ideas, and then strategize your next round of research.

B. Culture

1. What type of clothing was popular at this time? What were some popular recreational activities? What was the American diet like?

_____

_____

_____

2. What was important to the American people during this decade? What movements or revolutions occurred at this time?

_____

3. What were some of the popular sayings or slang in this decade?

_____

Notes: _____

_____

_____

_____

_____

C. Literature

1. What were the popular stories or written works at this time? Who were some famous American authors?

_____

2. Which authors won the Pulitzer Prize for fiction during this decade?

_____

3. Which books were made into popular movies?

_____

Notes: _____

_____

_____

_____

_____

HISTORY NOTEBOOK | THE STORY OF A DECADE
Research and Data

Now that you've done more research, what are you learning? Meet with your group to discuss. Now may also be a good time to see if there are any changes your group wants to make to your presentation format. Once you all agree, then continue with your research.

D. Art

1. What were the popular museum exhibitions during this time?

_____

2. Who were the popular artists? What were some famous works of art?

_____

3. What type of music was most popular? What were some popular dances?

_____

Notes: _____

_____

_____

_____

_____

E. Economics

1. What was the state of the economy at the time?

_____

2. What was the unemployment rate?

_____

3. What major news stories were published about the economy?

_____

_____

Notes: _____

_____

_____

_____

_____

HISTORY NOTEBOOK | THE STORY OF A DECADE
Create Your Presentation

You've researched and found information about your decade. Now it's time to regroup and create your final presentation. Review the steps below, answer the questions, and then use the spaces below to draft the presentation.

A. Project Presentation

1. Organize your information on each aspect for your decade.

2. Be sure to include maps, graphs, photographs, or other visuals to illustrate the story of your decade.

3. Prepare any other tools you need for the actual presentation. Do you need a computer? A screen? A bulletin board or poster board? What other items do you need?

4. Create a written list of all group members and what each group member did.

5. Make sure your presentation is interactive.

6. Presentations should take a minimum of 10 minutes, with an additional 5 minutes to set up, if needed.

B. Your Decade What story did your decade tell about American life?

_____

_____

_____

_____

_____

_____

_____

_____

_____

_____

_____

C. How did events and ideas from your chosen decade affect life as you know it today?

_____

_____

_____

_____

_____

_____

 **HISTORY NOTEBOOK** THE STORY OF A DECADE
After Your Final Presentation

 **NATIONAL GEOGRAPHIC** L E A R N I N G

You did it! You told the story of your decade—and heard other stories as well.
Review and answer the questions below.

1. What themes did you notice across decades?

_____

_____

_____

_____

2. What major changes did you notice over the decades? What stayed the same over the years?

_____

_____

_____

_____

3. Which decade do you think most affected life as you know it today? How so?

_____

_____

_____

_____

Record any other thoughts or notes on your project and what you learned below.

Notes: _____

_____

_____

_____

_____

_____

_____

_____

_____

_____

_____

HISTORY NOTEBOOK

PROJECTS FOR INQUIRY-BASED LEARNING
Documenting History

NATIONAL GEOGRAPHIC
L E A R N I N G

As you've been reading about U.S. history, you've learned about moments in history that have influenced the American experience today. These moments—key events—tell the stories about how our nation came to be, as we know it today. For this project, you will use digital storytelling to dig deeper into a pivotal event in history and answer essential questions about U.S. history.

DIRECTIONS AND REQUIREMENTS: You will work in a small group of two or three. Each group will choose an event in U.S. history to research. For the group's selected event, they must choose an overarching question to answer in their digital stories. Each group will present their research in the form of a documentary-style video. As a group, you will share your completed video with the class to provide a digital story of the event.

Remember, your video is your own personal documentary that can preserve the story of a historical event in your own words.

A. Project Steps Take a look at the steps below before you get started.

1. Get into your group.

2. Decide as a group what historical event you will research, and develop the key question you want to explore related to that event.

3. Research your selected historical event. Identify the key players, the setting, and the most interesting facts. Your research will also include finding appropriate images, videos, and music for your overall video. Include speeches, quotes, photographs, illustrations, maps, and models to tell the story of the historical event.

4. Plan your video—think about what you will illustrate and the information you want to get across. The best way to begin is to create an outline and put your video in order. Planning will help you iron out the details. Also, when planning, decide who will be responsible for which tasks.

5. Gather any tools you will need to record your video.

6. Finally, produce your video. Be as creative as you like and have fun!

B. Project Requirements The requirements listed below will help give you a general framework for the project.

1. The overarching question guides your analysis and research and should be understandable, relevant, and constructive.

2. Key information is provided about your selected event, and the main question is clearly answered.

3. Visuals and media selected tell a cohesive story and flow in an organized way.

4. Use a minimum of three credible resources for research. Be sure to include a works-cited credits page at the end of your video.

5. Permission is obtained for anyone participating in the video.

6. If you choose to use a location for your video, select one location only. Be sure to get permission to use the location before you start recording.

7. All group members participate in the research and creation of the project. Be sure to identify who was responsible for each task.

8. Presentation and narration are original, clear, appropriate, and organized. Visuals are appropriate to the topic.

9. Final presentation must be a complete video, between 3 to 4 minutes in length.

Name _____

Planning is key to making a video. You can't always go back and re-shoot something. Since you're making a 3- to 4-minute video, it's important to break it down into segments to focus on each part and work efficiently. Use an outline to organize each scene. Your outline can also serve as your script.

A. Conduct Research Before you can create your outline or script, you need to research your event and answer some questions to help decide the focus of your video. Respond to the questions below, and conduct any additional research needed. You may want to record research notes in your notebook.

1. What historical event are you researching? From what time period?

_____

2. What is your guiding, or key, question you are addressing in your documentary?

_____

3. Who were the key historical figures involved in this event?

_____

4. Why did you choose the event you selected to research? What interesting or surprising facts can you include about the event?

_____

_____

B. Plan the Details There are several details to think about as you plan your documentary. From narration to visuals, you will need to decide what works best for your video. Use the questions below to help you iron out the details.

5. What point do you want to get across? What do you want to illustrate?

_____

6. Which visuals or media will you use to convey your digital story? How do they answer the key question?

_____

_____

7. Who will narrate the video? Will the narrator be on-camera or off-camera as a voiceover?

_____

8. What graphics, if any, do you need and what will the graphics say?

_____

9. Where will you record your video? What tools will you need to record and produce your video?

_____

10. How will you pace your video? Will you tell the story in chronological order or mix it up?

_____

HISTORY NOTEBOOK | DOCUMENTING HISTORY
Outline Your Video

You finished your research, and your group got together to plan out the details. Now you're ready to take all your notes and prepare an outline, which will also serve as the video script. You can draft your outline in the two-column format below, or copy the format on to your own paper to write your script. In the left-hand column, write down what the visuals will be for that particular segment, or scene. Then in the right-hand column, write the audio that will go along with that scene.

VIDEO	AUDIO
Example: Graphic of the key question: How did the Great Depression affect the U.S. economy, and how has it influenced the nation today?	*Example:* How did the Great Depression affect the U.S. economy, and how has it influenced the nation today? In order to answer these questions, we need to first look at the factors that led to the Great Depression.

Name _____

The planning is done, the script is written, the narrator is good to go, the visuals are ready, and you have your story. All the permissions needed are set. You're ready to record!

A. Record and Assemble Your Video Use this quick checklist to help you record and put together all the parts of your digital story.

☐ All permissions requests submitted.

☐ Camera or smartphone prepped and ready to record video. Make sure the battery is charged. Test the audio and video quality.

☐ Gather the narrator and crew. Make sure everyone knows their roles and they are familiar with the script.

☐ Check that the location is ready and all props and visuals are set up or nearby to use when needed.

☐ Add any music and additional graphics to your video.

B. Your Documenting History Video Your video is complete, and it's time to turn it in and share it with the class. Be sure to submit a written list of all group members and what each group member did when you turn in your video.

1. What did you learn from this project?

_____

_____

_____

_____

2. What do you get from a documentary video that you don't get from a written version of the event?

_____

_____

_____

_____

3. What went well with your project, and what challenges did you encounter?

_____

_____

_____

4. What was the general reaction of your class or friends when you shared your video?

_____

_____

_____

HISTORY NOTEBOOK | ACTIVE CITIZENSHIP
Student Activism

NATIONAL GEOGRAPHIC LEARNING

History is full of movements led by students. From the fight for civil rights to the protests against the Dakota Access Pipeline, young adults from around the world have moved social change forward. When youth activists have agency, or the capacity to exert power, and they come together for a common cause, the effect of their collective voices can be a compelling force for change.

After students at Marjory Stoneman Douglas High School faced a tragic shooting in their school in 2018, they came together to demand gun reforms and to end school shootings. They joined forces with other students around the country who also wanted to put an end to gun violence.

In what became one of the most ambitious demonstrations from a student-led movement, on March 24, 2018, hundreds of thousands of people gathered for the March for Our Lives protest in Washington, D.C. and across the country in a call for action against gun violence.

©Ethan Miller/Getty Images

On March 24, 2018, students gathered in cities across the United States and around the world to join March for Our Lives events for school safety from guns.

1. **Make Inferences** Why do young people get involved in social movements? Do you think that they should get involved or stay out of it? Explain your reasoning.

_____

_____

_____

_____

2. **Identify** What are some common methods of student activism?

_____

_____

_____

_____

3. **Analyze Cause and Effect** What are the benefits of student activism? What are the drawbacks?

_____

_____

_____

HISTORY NOTEBOOK

ACTIVE CITIZENSHIP
Student Activism

NATIONAL GEOGRAPHIC
L E A R N I N G

4. Evaluate How has student activism evolved with the use of social media?

_____

_____

_____

5. What do you think are the best ways to get others to join a cause? How would you get people to join your cause?

_____

_____

_____

6. Conduct research on a successful protest. What made it successful? What actions were taken and what did those actions lead to? Record your notes below and also explain why this particular protest stood out to you.

_____

_____

_____

_____

_____

_____

©Craig Hudson/ASSOCIATED PRESS

As part of the March for Our Lives protest, students rally on the steps of the Capitol building in Charleston, West Virginia to address school safety and gun violence.

© National Geographic Learning, a Cengage Company

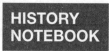

ACTIVE CITIZENSHIP

Putting Your Voice into Action

What issues matter to you? Maybe you care about the environment or you want to protect a historic building in your community. As a citizen, you have a voice. Think about ways in which you can become an engaged and responsible citizen.

1. **Form and Support Opinions** What do you think are the rights and responsibilities of a citizen? Explain your reasoning.

_____

_____

_____

_____

2. **Identify Problems and Solutions** What are some of the key issues in the United States today? What do you think are key issues or problems in your community, neighborhood, or school?

_____

_____

_____

_____

_____

_____

3. **Evaluate** Of the issues you listed above, what are you most passionate about and why? Think about a cause you would choose to support.

_____

_____

_____

_____

4. Take some time to conduct online research on your cause or topic. Identify what the cause or issue is, and find out if others are supporting the same cause. Read more about the topic, and explain why it's important. Be sure to identify both sides of the cause to understand different perspectives. Use the space below for your notes.

_____

_____

_____

_____

_____

HISTORY NOTEBOOK ACTIVE CITIZENSHIP
Putting Your Voice into Action

5. Once you've learned more about the topic, find out what work has already been done or is currently being done on the issue. Write your notes below.

_____

_____

_____

_____

_____

_____

6. Identify What resources already exist in support of your topic? Make a list of resources, such as groups or websites, you can tap into.

_____

_____

_____

_____

7. Describe Think about what ways you could support your cause or issue. What action are you hoping to encourage? Describe the goals you want to achieve.

_____

_____

_____

_____

_____

8. Now that you've set your goals, think about the steps you would need to take to meet those goals. Create your action plan below and include ways to bring awareness to your cause.

_____

_____

_____

_____

_____

_____

_____

HISTORY NOTEBOOK | The Story of a Continent

Read **The Story of a Continent** and use the questions below to look through the lens of history, starting from the beginnings of civilization, and learn about the story of North America.

1. **Describe** What was the geology and landscape of North America like during the Pleistocene epoch? Describe life in North America at this time.

_____

_____

_____

_____

2. **Interpret Maps** The Clovis point was a tool used for hunting by early hunter-gatherers archaeologists called the Clovis Culture. Look at the map of the Clovis Point Discoveries. What does the location of the tools tell you about the development of the culture and people?

_____

_____

_____

_____

3. **Draw Conclusions** What conclusions can you draw about the role of agriculture in early North American societies?

_____

_____

_____

_____

4. The corn we eat today isn't the same as it was in the beginning. What other foods can be traced back to early civilization? Do some online research to find another type of popular food we use today and trace its evolution. Prepare a short presentation on your findings. Be creative—use a map like the one in your textbook or use other visuals.

_____

_____

_____

_____

 **The Story of a Continent**

5. Form and Support Opinions The cultural mosaic of the United States is diverse. Do you agree with the statement that "diversity is one of the best things in life in the United States"? Why or why not?

_____

_____

_____

_____

_____

_____

_____

6. Ask Questions The history of the United States doesn't start with the Revolutionary War—it can be traced back to the earliest days before human beings roamed North America. Before you begin reading the chapters in this program, write a couple of questions you have about the beginnings of civilization in North America.

_____

_____

_____

_____

_____

_____

_____

7. Through the Lens As this feature notes, everyone has a personal American story to tell. What is your personal American Story? If you were to "look through the lens" of your family's origins, what would you learn? What do you know about your family's history? Try to trace back as much of your family history as possible, and write the story of how and when they came to the United States.

_____

_____

_____

_____

_____

_____

_____

Before the Europeans arrived in North American, Cahokia was at one time a great city—how did it come to be and what led to the city's demise? Find out in this American Story, and then respond to the questions below.

1. **Reading Check** What is Monks Mound and why is it significant?

_____

_____

_____

_____

2. **Summarize** Use your own words to summarize how the city of Cahokia developed.

_____

_____

_____

_____

3. **Describe** Write two descriptions of Cahokia: one based on the artist's rendering shown and one based on the photographs of Cahokia today. Pair up with a partner and trade descriptions. To what extent were your descriptions similar? How did your impressions vary?

_____

_____

_____

_____

4. **Draw Conclusions** Based on what you learned, what conclusions can you make about the downfall of Cahokia?

_____

_____

_____

5. **Synthesize** Archaeologists work to uncover clues about past cultures. What have archaeologists' findings at Cahokia told us about early life in the United States?

_____

_____

_____

NATIONAL GEOGRAPHIC EXPLORER SARAH PARCAK
Space, Satellites, and Archaeology

National Geographic Explorer and space archaeologist Sarah Parcak uses new technology not only to uncover lost civilizations but also to find evidence of looting at archaeological sites. Read about her innovative work, and then answer the questions below.

1. **Reading Check** What advantages does satellite technology provide archaeologists that traditional methods might not?

_____

_____

_____

2. What aspects of Parcak's work do you find most interesting? Would you want to do what Parcak does for a living? Why or why not?

_____

_____

_____

3. **Describe** How does satellite technology help identify sites that have been looted?

_____

_____

_____

4. **Ask Questions** Imagine you get to interview Sarah Parcak for your school website or local newspaper. What are three important questions you want to ask her?

_____

_____

_____

5. **Turn and Talk** Parcak uses satellite technology to investigate archaeological sites. Discuss with a partner other types of technology that could be used to help archaeologists in their work. What current technology or devices could be used to find out more about ancient civilizations? How do you think those devices could be used? Discuss your ideas, and record your notes below.

_____

_____

_____

_____

_____

HISTORY NOTEBOOK **UNIT 1** *REID ON THE ROAD*
Map of a Pizza

After you watch the video, answer the questions below.

1. Identify What was the single fact about pizza that surprised you the most? Why was it surprising?

_____

_____

_____

_____

2. Explain What part of the story of pizza did you find most interesting? Write a few sentences to explain. What do you want to find out more about?

_____

_____

_____

_____

3. The people interviewed on the video all like different kinds of pizza. Do a little research to determine how pizza can be made in healthy ways. What choices can help change pizza from an unhealthy snack to a healthy choice for dinner?

_____

_____

_____

_____

4. Form and Support Opinions Do you think the Columbian Exchange was important? If so, why? If not, why not?

_____

_____

_____

_____

5. Pizza isn't the only food that originated somewhere else and then came to North America. What other foods can you think of that originally came from other countries? Think of some examples, such as kimchi, tacos, and French fries. Pick one food and do some online research to map its path to North America. Be prepared to talk about your selected food with the class. Record your notes below.

_____

_____

_____

_____

AMERICAN GALLERY
Early American Civilizations

Learn about early American civilizations in this American Gallery. After reviewing the photographs, answer the questions below.

1. Evaluate Of the artifacts shown in this gallery, which did you find most interesting and why?

_____

_____

_____

2. Use your own words to explain what these photographs as a group reveal about early American civilizations.

_____

_____

_____

3. Describe Select one of the three sites shown in this gallery, and study the photography closely. Describe the site as you would to someone unable to view the photograph. What adjectives would you use? What details would you include in your description of the site, city, or structures?

_____

_____

_____

_____

4. Draw Conclusions What conclusions can you draw about the technology and craftsmanship of early American civilizations based on the photographs in this gallery?

_____

_____

_____

5. Imagine it's 200 years from now, and identify objects from your life today that you think best represents technology and artistry in modern society. Think about how it would help future generations understand current American civilization. List the objects below and explain what you think each objects reveals about American society today.

_____

_____

_____

_____

_____

HISTORY NOTEBOOK | UNIT **1** | AMERICAN STORY
The Colony of Jamestown

NATIONAL GEOGRAPHIC
L E A R N I N G

Learn more about the well-known story of Jamestown and the first colonists who settled there. Then explore your understanding by answering the questions below.

1. **Reading Check** How did the Jamestown settlers change the land there? What factors led to the changes?

_____

_____

_____

2. **Summarize** What was the Jamestown settlers' relationship like with the local Native Americans?

_____

_____

_____

3. **Analyze Primary Sources** Review the excerpt from the "Nova Britannia" pamphlet. What "selling points" does it make to promote the colony?

_____

_____

_____

4. **Evaluate** Think about the factors the Jamestown settlers had to consider when choosing a new place to live. Imagine you were leading a group of settlers coming to America. Who would you bring? Where you would want to settle and why? What factors would be most important to consider for your new settlement?

_____

_____

_____

_____

5. **Discuss and Debate** Author Charles C. Mann notes, "Four centuries ago, the English didn't discover a New World—they created one." Form a group with three other classmates and discuss his quote. Then stage a quick debate about whether the Jamestown settlers should have created their own world or acclimated to the existing environment. Have two of you argue one side and the other two argue the other side. Record notes for each argument below.

_____

_____

_____

_____

HISTORY NOTEBOOK | **UNIT 1** | *REID ON THE ROAD*
Plimouth Plantation

Did pilgrims really dress the way we think they did? Find out the answer as National Geographic Digital Nomad Robert Reid goes to Plimouth Plantation in Plymouth, Massachusetts. Then review the questions below and record your responses.

1. **Ask and Answer Questions** Before watching the video, write three questions you have about pilgrims. List the questions below, and then after you watch the video, record the answers. Were all your questions answered? If so, what other questions do you have? If not, do some research to find out the answers.

_____

_____

_____

2. What single fact related to the pilgrims' or Native Americans' outfits surprised you the most?

_____

_____

_____

3. **Explore Identity** What does the clothing in the paintings of pilgrims reveal about their identity? What does the clothing the pilgrims actually wore say about their identity?

_____

_____

_____

4. **Connect to Today** Like it or not, one of the first things people notice about others is what they are wearing. Write a sentence that connects the clothes we wear today with the concept of identity.

_____

_____

_____

5. How does the video help you understand pilgrim life and Thanksgiving?

_____

_____

_____

6. **Make Inferences** What does the video tell you about stereotypes? Why do you think people form stereotypes about someone or something?

_____

_____

_____

NATIONAL GEOGRAPHIC EXPLORER
William Kelso

National Geographic Explorer and archaeologist William Kelso has been working over 20 years to uncover the truth about America's first settlement. His findings have told us more about the story of Jamestown. Find out what he's discovered and answer the questions below.

1. **Reading Check** How has the way people viewed Jamestown changed based on the evidence William Kelso has found to date?

_____

_____

_____

2. What aspects of Kelso's work do you find most interesting? Would you want to do what Kelso does for a living? Why or why not?

_____

_____

_____

3. **Analyze Language Use** What did Kelso mean when he said, "That's when liberty got out of the bag, and nobody could stuff it back in"?

_____

_____

_____

_____

4. **Turn and Talk** Think about the factors the Jamestown settlers had to consider when choosing a new place to live. Imagine you were an English settler coming to America. Discuss with a partner where you would want to settle and why. What factors would be most important to consider for your new settlement? Record your notes below.

_____

_____

_____

5. **Form and Support Opinions** Kelso says that Jamestown is where America first began. Do you agree with that statement? Why or why not? Support your answer with evidence from the text.

_____

_____

_____

_____

HISTORY NOTEBOOK | UNIT **1** | AMERICAN GALLERY
Southern Plantations

NATIONAL
GEOGRAPHIC
L E A R N I N G

Go online to view this American Gallery about southern plantations and the lives of enslaved people who worked there. Then respond to the questions below.

1. **Evaluate** Which photograph or painting in this gallery do you find most interesting. Explain why.

_____

_____

_____

2. **Explore Identity** What do you think these images as a group convey about American identity?

_____

_____

_____

3. **Describe** How would you describe the architectural style of the structures found on southern plantations? What does the style tell you about the style of the South?

_____

_____

_____

_____

4. **Make Connections** How do the photographs in this gallery demonstrate the ways enslaved people lived and were treated?

_____

_____

_____

5. Select one of the buildings shown in this gallery. Then conduct online research to learn more about that building and the plantation. Prepare a 3-minute presentation about the plantation, the building, and those who lived and worked there. Record your notes below.

_____

_____

_____

_____

_____

HISTORY NOTEBOOK | **UNIT 1** | AMERICAN STORY ONLINE
Colliding Cultures—The Fur Trade

Learn about how clothing and trade affected Native American cultures in this American Story. Then record your thoughts on the questions below.

1. **Reading Check** What common themes do you notice in this American Story?

_____

_____

_____

_____

2. **Form and Support Opinions** Do you agree that fashion affects our lives? If so, how? If not, why not?

_____

_____

_____

_____

3. While trade with the Europeans provided Native Americans with goods that helped make their lives easier and convenient, it sometimes was at a cost to their culture. What do you think is more important: having conveniences and new technology or maintaining traditions and culture? Explain your answer.

_____

_____

_____

_____

4. **Explore Identity** Beaver hats were a popular clothing item for Europeans. What did that fashion item say about their identity? How would you describe the idea of identity as expressed in fashion?

_____

_____

_____

_____

5. What are some popular clothing items today? Imagine it's 200 years from now, and identify a clothing item from your life today that you think would help future generations understand American life as you know it. List the clothing item below. Explain what you think it reveals about American life today.

_____

_____

HISTORY NOTEBOOK UNIT **1** AMERICAN VOICES
Olaudah Equiano

Read about abolitionist and writer Olaudah Equiano and his journey from enslavement to freedom. Then record your responses to the questions below.

1. Reading Check What is controversial about Olaudah Equiano's early life and why?

_____

_____

_____

2. Identify What role did Equiano play in the abolitionist movement?

_____

_____

_____

3. Ask and Answer Questions What question would you most like to ask Equiano if you met him right now? And how do you imagine he would answer?

_____

_____

_____

4. Equiano's called his autobiography an "interesting narrative of [his] life." The theme that seems central to his narrative is salvation. What would be an interesting narrative of your life? Think about what you would want people to remember about you and what your theme might be. Then write a brief autobiography of your life below.

_____

_____

_____

_____

_____

_____

_____

_____

_____

_____

Name _____

Explore the different rooms and structures of the Whitney Plantation and then answer the questions below.

1. Reading Check What is the Whitney Plantation and what is its goal?

_____

_____

_____

2. Make Inferences Why do you think the Whitney Plantation was made into a museum?

_____

_____

_____

3. Review the photographs and captions. What is your initial reaction to the photos and what you learned? How does what you learn from the Whitney Plantation change or reinforce your understanding of slavery?

_____

_____

_____

_____

4. Make Connections How do the photographs of the Whitney Plantation demonstrate the ways enslaved people lived and were treated?

_____

_____

_____

_____

5. The Whitney Plantation tells the story about the history and experiences of enslaved people in the United States. What story would you want to tell about U.S. history and people's experiences? Think about events or issues that impact the United States today. Imagine it's 100 years from now, and identify objects, photographs, or places from current day that you think will tell the history of today. What would people 100 years from now see?

_____

_____

_____

_____

Name

Go online to view this American Gallery featuring colonial landmarks and respond to the questions below.

1. **Make Connections** How do the photographs in this American Gallery help you understand what colonial life was like? What do the photos tell you about the American experience during colonial times?

_____

_____

_____

_____

2. **Compare and Contrast** Review the photographs and captions of colonial buildings. How are they similar, and how are the structures different? How would you describe colonial architecture?

_____

_____

_____

_____

3. **Evaluate** What do you learn from a photograph of colonial landmarks that you wouldn't learn from a written description of the same landmarks?

_____

_____

_____

_____

4. Study the photographs of the gravestones. Each one features a specific design or motif that symbolized colonial beliefs at that time. Think about American culture and society today. Design a gravestone with a decoration or motif you think symbolizes American culture today. Describe or draw your gravestone design below.

_____

_____

_____

_____

_____

_____

HISTORY NOTEBOOK | UNIT **1** | **UNIT WRAP-UP**
Settling a New World

NATIONAL GEOGRAPHIC
L E A R N I N G

This unit, Settling a New World, discusses the new colonies of early America settled by those who left Europe seeking a better way of life. Use the questions below to think about what you learned in Unit 1.

A. After Reading Once you've completed Unit 1, revisit the chapters to select the topic that you find most interesting.

1. What is the topic I found most interesting in this unit?

_____

2. How or why does this topic interest me?

_____

3. What are some of the most important take-aways you got from this unit?

_____

_____

4. How does this topic relate to my life, my family, my community, and my identity?

_____

_____

_____

B. Colonial New York Review the article and respond to the questions below.

5. What is the subject of the article?

_____

6. What does the online collection of city ordinances tell you about colonial New York? Why might documents such as city ordinances be important to historians?

_____

_____

_____

7. How does this article connect with the focus of the unit? Why do you think the editors of this U.S. History program selected this article for this unit?

_____

_____

_____

C. Unit Activities As you prepare for your unit inquiry and the learning framework, record any thoughts, ideas, or lingering questions below.

_____

_____

HISTORY NOTEBOOK | **UNIT 2** | **AMERICAN STORY ONLINE**
Daily Life During the Revolution

What was life like in colonial America? And how different was it than life today? Learn about everyday life in the colonies during the Revolution, and then answer the questions below.

1. **Reading Check** What role did education and religion play in colonial life?

_____

_____

_____

2. **Identify** What fact were you most surprised to learn about daily life in the colonies? Why?

_____

_____

_____

3. **Categorize** What social groups existed within colonial life? How would you categorize social groups today?

_____

_____

_____

4. **Compare and Contrast** Pick one aspect of daily life featured in this American Story and compare it with today. First, describe what that aspect is like today and then explain what you think is similar to and what is different from that aspect during the American Revolution.

_____

_____

_____

5. **Connect to Today** This American Story features a few selected rules from the book *Rules of Civility & Decent Behaviour In Company and Conversation*. Do you agree with these rules? Why or why not? What rules would you put in place for "civilized behavior" today? List at least three rules you think are the most important.

_____

_____

_____

_____

HISTORY NOTEBOOK | UNIT **2** | *REID ON THE ROAD*
Myths of 1776

NATIONAL GEOGRAPHIC
L E A R N I N G

There are many stories about the American Revolution—some are true and some are myths. Learn about one well-known story, and find out whether it's fact or fiction.

1. Evaluate After watching the video, what were you most surprised to learn?

_____

_____

_____

2. Make Inferences How do you think Paul Revere felt on his midnight ride? Is that an experience you would want to be a part of? Why or why not?

_____

_____

_____

_____

3. Paul Revere wasn't the only rider to Concord, but he is the most well known of the riders. In fact, as the video notes, there is even a poem written about him by Henry Wadsworth Longfellow called "Paul Revere's Ride." Watch the video again to listen to the line quoted from the poem. Conduct online research to find and read the rest of the poem. Then create a short poem for one of the other two riders mentioned in the video, either Samuel Prescott or William Dawes.

_____

_____

_____

_____

_____

4. Do you agree that myths "help keep these stories alive?" Why or why not?

_____

_____

_____

5. Fact vs. Myth Come up with two facts about the American Revolution, and then create one myth about the American Revolution. Share your two facts and a myth with a partner. See if your partner can identify the myth. Then reverse roles, have your partner share two different facts and a myth, and try to identify the myth. Take notes below on your selected facts and myth.

_____

_____

_____

HISTORY NOTEBOOK | **UNIT 2** | **THROUGH THE LENS, AMERICAN PLACES**
Boston Common

NATIONAL GEOGRAPHIC
L E A R N I N G

The oldest public park in the United States, Boston Common evolved throughout history. Study the photograph, text, and caption, and then respond to the questions below.

1. Reading Check Over the course of history, what purposes has Boston Common served?

_____

_____

2. Make Inferences Why do you think Boston Common endured throughout history?

_____

_____

_____

3. Describe Based on the photograph, how would you describe Boston Common? Go online to find more photos of Boston Common today and then add to your description of the park.

_____

_____

_____

4. Draw Conclusions Why might it be important to preserve nature within crowded cities?

_____

_____

_____

5. Compare and Contrast Conduct online research to find photographs, sketches, and illustrations of Boston Common through history. Create a photo gallery showing the evolution of the park over the years and compare the park in the past to the park today, from how it looks to how the area was used. Record your notes below.

_____

_____

_____

_____

6. Create a park for the community you live in. Think about how the park would be used, what you would want in your park, and how you would want it to look. Write your plan and the name of your park below.

_____

_____

_____

_____

HISTORY NOTEBOOK | UNIT 2

REID ON THE ROAD

Crossing the Delaware

Emanuel Leutze's painting *Washington Crossing the Delaware* is one of the most famous paintings in the United States. Why is this painting so iconic? What was the big deal about Washington's crossing? Find out why when you watch the video, and then answer the questions below.

1. **Describe** What do you think when you look at Leutze's painting of Washington crossing the Delaware River? What is your initial reaction to the painting?

_____

_____

_____

2. Imagine you were one of Washington's troops crossing the Delaware that night. What do you think it would have been like to cross the river? Consider the time of day, weather conditions, resources, and tasks. Write a few sentences below describing what the experience must have been like.

_____

_____

_____

3. **Form and Support Opinions** Do you think Washington's plan to cross the Delaware River was important to the American Revolution? Why or why not? What if he had failed—would that have made a difference? Explain your reasoning.

_____

_____

_____

4. In the video, the narrator and the George Washington character discuss what is inaccurate about the painting. Why do you think the artist chose to portray the crossing the way he did, even with the inaccuracies?

_____

_____

_____

5. **Draw Conclusions** How does the video help you understand the experience of crossing the Delaware River during the American Revolution? What does it tell you about George Washington?

_____

_____

_____

6. What did you find most interesting about this video? Explain why below.

_____

_____

Learn about the Battle of Long Island from battle re-enactors. After watching the video, respond to the questions and record your thoughts below.

1. **Identify** What new fact or information about American history did you learn from this video that you didn't already know or learn from your textbook?

_____

_____

2. **Turn and Talk** The narrator says, "Sometimes things don't happen as planned," and then gives a few examples of events gone wrong. Can you think of other historical events that didn't go as planned? Discuss with a partner and come up with at least two more examples. List them below and describe what went wrong.

_____

_____

_____

3. **Form and Support Opinions** After watching the video, do you consider the Battle of Long Island a failure or a success? Explain your answer.

_____

_____

_____

4. Re-enactors are people who dress up in the time period's costume and act out events from history. Would you want to be a re-enactor? Why or why not? If you would want to be a re-enactor, which historical event would you want to act out?

_____

_____

_____

5. The re-enactor in this video says, "This story doesn't get remembered unless we do what we are doing." How does the story of the Battle of Long Island contribute to the American Revolution? Do you think the story is worth remembering? Explain your answer.

_____

_____

_____

6. **Ask Questions** What more do you want to know about the Battle of Long Island? Write three questions you still have after watching the video.

_____

_____

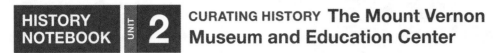

HISTORY NOTEBOOK | **UNIT 2** | CURATING HISTORY **The Mount Vernon Museum and Education Center**

Examine artifacts and objects found at the Mount Vernon Museum and Education Center and then respond to the prompts below.

1. **Reading Check** What type of museum is the Mount Vernon Museum and Education Center, and what does it showcase?

_____

_____

2. **Draw Conclusions** What do personal objects or clothing such as Martha Washington's gown tell you about American life? Why would it be important to preserve such items?

_____

_____

_____

3. **Identify** Knowing what you know about George Washington, what other objects would you add to this collection that would provide more insight about his life?

_____

_____

_____

4. **Form and Support Opinions** Some museums and some artifacts don't appeal to everyone, and that's to be expected. Would you want to visit this museum to see these objects? If so, why? If not, why not?

_____

_____

_____

5. Presidential libraries and museums can be found across the country. Choose one president and conduct online research to find out more about his museum. Explore the museum's website to find and select objects that you curate into a collection you think best conveys key points in your selected president's life. Record your notes below and explain why you chose the objects you did.

_____

_____

_____

_____

_____

Name _____

Explore this collection of photographs detailing Valley Forge. Then capture what you learned using the prompts below.

1. **Evaluate** What do you learn from photographs of Valley Forge that you wouldn't learn from a written description of the area?

_____

_____

2. Which photograph or painting from this gallery did you find most interesting and why?

_____

_____

3. **Make Inferences** Study the painting of George Washington at Valley Forge. How would you describe life and the conditions at Valley Forge? What might life have been like there for the soldiers?

_____

_____

_____

_____

4. **Turn and Talk** Most of the soldiers did not leave Valley Forge. They stayed even though the conditions were bad and the winter was tough. Why would they stay? Would you have left or stayed? Discuss your thoughts with a partner, and explain your reasoning. Record your notes below.

_____

_____

_____

_____

5. Create your own gallery to tell the story of Valley Forge. Start by picking one photograph and caption from this gallery, and then add at least three more photos you found about Valley Forge. Write captions for your photos.

_____

_____

_____

_____

_____

_____

HISTORY NOTEBOOK | UNIT **2** | AMERICAN STORY ONLINE
The Northwest Ordinances

Go online to study the Northwest Ordinances that helped create the advancement of democracy as the United States expanded westward. Reflect on what you learned below.

---

1. **Reading Check** What were the three Northwest Ordinances, and why were they created?

_____

_____

_____

_____

---

2. **Identify** How did the ordinance of 1784 set a precedent, and what was that precedent?

_____

_____

_____

_____

3. **Form and Support Opinions** Thomas Jefferson originally had a different plan for how the Northwest Territory would be divided but it was rejected. Do you agree with the new division of the territories created by Congress? Which states do you think were "winners" and which ones were "losers"? Explain your reasoning.

_____

_____

_____

_____

4. **Draw Conclusions** Why is the ordinance of 1787 considered the most important?

_____

_____

_____

_____

5. **Turn and Talk** Form a group with three other classmates. Have each person in the group pick one state: Illinois, Michigan, Ohio, or Wisconsin. Imagine that you are each a legislator from your selected state and present your petition to become a state, outlining your borders and why you think those borders work best. Record your notes below.

_____

_____

_____

AMERICAN GALLERY
Crafting the Constitution

Review the photographs in this American Gallery, and then answer the questions below.

1. **Explore Identity** What do these visuals as a group tell you about the American identity during the late 1700s as well as today?

_____

_____

_____

2. **Identify** After studying the photographs and captions, what fact or idea related to the constitution most surprised you? What was surprising about it?

_____

_____

_____

_____

3. **Make Generalizations** Study the photograph of the sun carving on Washington's chair. What generalizations can you make about the craftsmanship of this object?

_____

_____

_____

_____

4. **Connect to Today** The inkstand used by the signers of the Declaration of Independence and the U.S. Constitution is one of the most historically significant objects preserved from this momentous time. Think about a current event today that you think is significant. What one object from this event do you think would best represent the importance of the event? Explain your reasoning.

_____

_____

_____

5. **Form and Support Opinions** What do you think were the main ideas and goals of the delegates during the crafting of the constitution? Do you think those ideals have changed or stayed the same throughout history? If yes, how? If no, why not?

_____

_____

_____

HISTORY NOTEBOOK | UNIT **2** | AMERICAN STORY
The Founding Fathers

Who were the leaders behind the establishment and growth of the United States? Find out more about them in this American Story, and then answer the questions below.

---

1. **Reading Check** Who were the some of the leading Founding Fathers, and why were they referred to as such?

_____

_____

_____

---

2. **Make Generalizations** What common qualities do you notice among the three Founding Fathers featured in this American Story? Based on those qualities, what generalization can you make about their leadership?

_____

_____

_____

3. Who or what did you find most interesting in this American Story and why? What more would you like to know about that person, place, or object?

_____

_____

_____

4. **Form and Support Opinions** Each of these Founding Fathers were truly remarkable individuals. Support that statement with your own opinions about their accomplishments—or explain why you aren't all that impressed with them.

_____

_____

_____

_____

5. **Turn and Talk** Form a group with two other classmates and discuss the achievements of George Washington, Thomas Jefferson, and Benjamin Franklin. Who do you think had the greatest impact on the formation and growth of the United States? Support your opinion with evidence from the text.

_____

_____

_____

_____

NATIONAL GEOGRAPHIC L E A R N I N G

Watch this video on Thomas Jefferson's home, Monticello, and then respond to the prompts below.

1. **Form and Support Opinions** After watching this video on Thomas Jefferson and Monticello, what is your opinion of Jefferson? What did you learn about him that you didn't already know?

_____

_____

_____

2. Would you want to visit Monticello? Write a few sentences about why you might or might not want to do so.

_____

_____

_____

3. **Explore Identity** Jefferson wrote the words for his own gravestone. The achievements he listed are the ones he most identified with. Why do you think he didn't identify himself as President of the United States on his gravestone? What do you value, and how would you identify yourself?

_____

_____

_____

4. **Design Your Home** If you were the architect of your own home, what kind of home would you design? Consider the types of rooms you would need, the number of rooms, and the style of your home—on the inside as well as the outside. Would it be made of brick, wood, or other material? Would you want a modern style or traditional? Think also about whether you would like a room for one of your hobbies, such as a library for reading or an indoor court for basketball. Be creative—it can be whatever you want it to be. Write your description of your home below.

_____

_____

_____

_____

_____

_____

_____

_____

_____

NATIONAL GEOGRAPHIC
L E A R N I N G

Find out how people got around the country before planes, trains, and automobiles. Join Digital Nomad Robert Reid as he goes to New Orleans, Louisiana, and meets with Wendell Stout, a tour guide and historian of a genuine Mississippi River paddle wheeler.

1. **Describe** Have you been to any part of the Mississippi River? If so, how would you describe it? What were your impressions of the river? If not, how would you describe it based on the video?

_____

_____

_____

2. **Compare and Contrast** Compare your description with that of one of your classmates. What things about the Mississippi River did you see in a similar way? How did your impressions vary?

_____

_____

_____

3. Imagine you are a reporter in the 19th century reporting on Mississippi River steamboat travel. Write a news article the about river as transportation. Include an interview with Robert Fulton and Mr. Shreve. Record below the questions you would ask. Then write your article.

_____

_____

_____

_____

_____

4. **Connect to Today** If you had to travel from New Orleans, Louisiana to Minneapolis, Minnesota, today, would you want to travel by boat along the Mississippi River? If so, why? If not, why not and what other method would you want to travel by?

_____

_____

_____

5. After watching the video, what did you learn about the Mississippi River that you didn't already know? What more would you like to know?

_____

_____

_____

HISTORY NOTEBOOK | **UNIT 2** | **AMERICAN VOICES**
Sacagawea

Meriwether Lewis and William Clark and their Corps of Discovery explored new territory for the United States, but they couldn't have done it without one woman: Sacagawea. Learn about her life and the vital role she played in history, and then respond to the questions below.

1. **Reading Check** As the only woman on the team, how did Sacagawea come to join the expedition? In what ways did she serve the expedition?

_____

_____

_____

2. **Identify** What personal qualities did Sacagawea exhibit on this expedition? How did those qualities affect the expedition?

_____

_____

_____

3. **Make Predictions** What if Sacagawea was not on Lewis and Clark's expedition? What do you think would have happened on the trip? Would they have been successful or not?

_____

_____

_____

4. **Form and Support Opinions** Clark says, "A woman with a party of men is a token of peace." Do you think that's true? If so, why would that be the case? If not, why not?

_____

_____

_____

5. **Ask Questions** What questions would you most like to ask Sacagawea if you were face to face right now?

_____

_____

_____

6. Do you see Sacagawea as a role model? Is she someone you would try to emulate? If so, why? If not, why not?

_____

_____

HISTORY NOTEBOOK | **UNIT 2**

AMERICAN GALLERY
On the Trail with Lewis and Clark

NATIONAL GEOGRAPHIC
L E A R N I N G

Study the photographs in this American Gallery to learn about Lewis and Clark's expedition. Then respond to the prompts below.

1. **Make Inferences** How do the visuals in this American Gallery help you understand what Meriwether Lewis and William Clark's expedition was like? What do the photos tell you about the American experience?

_____

_____

_____

2. **Ask and Answer Questions** As you explore the gallery, write down three questions you have about the expedition. Then pair up with a partner, trade questions, and try to answer your partner's questions.

_____

_____

_____

3. **Describe** Select one photograph or painting to study closely. Describe the image as you would to someone unable to view it. What adjectives would you use? What details would you try to convey?

_____

_____

_____

4. **Evaluate** Pick one of the photos in this gallery and talk about it in terms of photographic technique. For example, is it a close-up or taken from a distance? Is there a certain angle that the photographer took that makes the photo special? What makes this particular photograph compelling or surprising?

_____

_____

_____

_____

5. Lewis and Clark both kept journals detailing their discoveries during their expedition. Imagine you are either Lewis or Clark and write a journal entry describing a new species or area from his perspective. Think about not only the description of what was discovered but also what his thoughts and reactions might have been.

_____

_____

_____

_____

_____

HISTORY NOTEBOOK | **UNIT 2**

UNIT WRAP-UP
Revolution and a New Nation

NATIONAL GEOGRAPHIC
L E A R N I N G

This unit, Revolution and a New Nation, describes how the United States came to be its own nation. Use the questions below to think about what you learned in Unit 2.

A. After Reading Once you've completed Unit 2, revisit the chapters to select the topic that you find most interesting.

1. What is the topic I found most interesting in this unit?

_____

2. How or why does this topic interest me?

_____

3. What are some of the most important take-aways you got from this unit?

_____

_____

4. How does this topic relate to my life, my family, my community, and my identity?

_____

_____

_____

B. Map Drawing Review the article and respond to the questions below.

5. What is the subject of the article?

_____

6. Why was map drawing a part of schoolwork for young girls? What skills did they develop as a result of drawing maps?

_____

_____

_____

7. How does this article connect with the focus of the unit? Why do you think the editors of this U.S. History program selected this article for this unit?

_____

_____

_____

C. Unit Activities As you prepare for your unit inquiry and the learning framework, record any thoughts, ideas, or lingering questions below.

_____

HISTORY NOTEBOOK | **UNIT 3** | AMERICAN STORY
American Inventions

Study this American Story to learn about some of the most noteworthy inventions in U.S. history that have changed our everyday lives. Then answer the questions below.

---

1. Reading Check What is the purpose of a patent, and how does an inventor go about getting one?

_____

_____

_____

---

2. Compare and Contrast The telegraph was once used for communication. How are communication tools similar to and different from the telegraph today? How will they be different or the same in the future?

_____

_____

_____

3. Identify What personal qualities does it take to be an inventor? Who is a 21st-century inventor you admire? Explain what you admire about him or her.

_____

_____

_____

_____

4. Form and Support Opinions Of the inventions featured in this American Story, which one do you think is the greatest invention and why?

_____

_____

_____

_____

5. Imagine its 200 years from now, and identify an invention from your life today that you think is one of the greatest inventions in modern society. Think about how it would help future generations understand American life. List below the invention you chose. Explain its significance and what you think it reveals about American life today.

_____

_____

_____

_____

HISTORY NOTEBOOK | UNIT **3** | NATIONAL GEOGRAPHIC EXPLORER
Kevin Crisman

What can past shipwrecks tell us about American life? Apparently a lot. National Geographic Explorer and underwater archaeologist Kevin Crisman's exploration of one steamboat, the *Heroine*, reveals new details about life during the heyday of steamboat transportation.

1. **Reading Check** What new information did Kevin Crisman and his team discover from their exploration of the *Heroine*?

_____

_____

_____

2. **Evaluate** Why was the process of excavating the *Heroine* challenging? How is underwater excavation different from land excavation?

_____

_____

_____

_____

3. What aspects of being an underwater archaeologist do you think you might find appealing? What might not be appealing? Explain your reasoning.

_____

_____

_____

_____

4. **Identify** What personal qualities do you think a person who does the work Kevin Crisman does would need to have? List three qualities and explain why they would be important.

_____

_____

_____

5. After reading this lesson, what were you most surprised to learn? What was most interesting to you and why?

_____

_____

_____

As the nation expanded, the fertile Great Lakes region drew in more and more people and businesses. Learn how this growth and development affected the landscape.

1. **Reading Check** What role did the Great Lakes region play during European exploration? What made it a good choice for that role?

_____

_____

_____

2. **Describe** Have you ever been to any of the Great Lakes? How would you describe the landscape to someone who hasn't been there? If you haven't been to any of the Great Lakes, which lake would you want to see and what would you want to know about it?

_____

_____

_____

3. **Identify Problems and Solutions** The text points out some problems caused by lakeshore development, such as pollution. Pick one of the problems mentioned—or think of one not already covered—and propose a solution to the problem. Write your solution below.

_____

_____

_____

4. **Make Predictions** How might the natural landscape around the Great Lakes change if the health of the Great Lakes region is not maintained? If human modifications continue? Consider positive and negative effects.

_____

_____

_____

5. Go online and find other photographs of the Great Lakes region or focus on one of the Great Lakes. Create a photo gallery of the specific lake or the Great Lakes region using at least 5 photos, and write captions to go with each photo. Be prepared to present your photo gallery to the class.

_____

_____

_____

_____

HISTORY NOTEBOOK | **UNIT 3** | *REID ON THE ROAD* **State Shapes**

NATIONAL GEOGRAPHIC
L E A R N I N G

Join Robert Reid as he travels to the National Geographic Society in Washington, D.C. There he meets with Dr. Fred Hiebert, National Geographic Archaeologist-in-Residence and Explorer, to talk about how states got their shapes.

1. **Analyze Visuals** What does Dr. Hiebert mean when he says, "you really could spend a lot of time just looking at the map and thinking, 'This is U.S. History'"? What does the map tell us about history?

_____

_____

_____

_____

2. **Ask Questions** National Geographic houses thousands of maps, and the cartographic department at the Society made many of them. What questions do you have for the cartographers who make the maps at National Geographic?

_____

_____

_____

3. **Form and Support Opinions** Some state borders were based on geographic features, while other state borders were based on math and space. Which way do you think is the best way to define a state's borders? Explain your answer.

_____

_____

_____

4. **Interpret Maps** Look at a map of the United States with state borders. What is your favorite state shape? Note your reasons below. Then form a group with 3 other classmates, and have each person share which state is his or her favorite and why. What do the chosen state shapes remind you of or look like?

_____

_____

_____

5. Find your state on a map. Draw the state shape below. Think about what Reid says about the shape of his state, Oklahoma. The shape tells a story about his state. How would you describe the shape of your state, and what story does it tell?

Your state shape:

HISTORY NOTEBOOK | UNIT **3** | AMERICAN GALLERY
Industrializing America

The first half of the 19th century saw rapid growth with new innovations that fueled major industries in the United States. This economic and industrial growth would lay the foundation for new technologies in the years to come.

1. Identify What does this gallery as a whole tell you about the American Industrial Revolution?

_____

_____

_____

_____

2. Evaluate Which photograph do you find most interesting or compelling and why?

_____

_____

_____

_____

_____

3. Draw Conclusions Why would the U.S. National Park Service preserve former industrial sites or buildings, such as Slater's Mill? What conclusions can you draw about the relevance of such sites?

_____

_____

_____

_____

_____

4. Make Connections How has the Industrial Revolution influenced American culture and identity today?

_____

_____

_____

_____

5. Discuss and Debate "Buy American!" was a slogan during the Industrial Revolution. Form a group with three other classmates and discuss the slogan and why it was significant in the early 19th century. Then stage a quick debate on whether this slogan should be the model for spending habits today. Have two of you argue the side for and the other two argue the side against this statement. Record notes for each argument below.

_____

_____

_____

How do you maintain your own identity when you are surrounded by change? How do you adapt to a new culture while retaining your family traditions and your individuality? These are some of the questions many Native Americans faced as the United States expanded—and still face today.

1. **Reading Check** Describe early Cherokee society.

_____

_____

_____

2. **Describe** How did Cherokee society evolve over time? Which aspects did they keep and which did they change?

_____

_____

_____

3. **Evaluate** What does this American Story tell you about Native American culture? Did what you learned change or reinforce your understanding of Native American history and culture? How so?

_____

_____

_____

_____

4. **Form and Support Opinions** In new or changing situations, is it better to maintain your own identity or assimilate into another group's culture? Explain your reasoning. How would you go about maintaining your identity or adopting elements of another culture?

_____

_____

_____

_____

5. **Discuss and Debate** As white settlement progressed, the Cherokee and other Native American groups were forced to move from their homes. Form a group with three other classmates and stage a quick debate on the following questions: How should the Cherokee have responded? And what responsibility did the U.S. government have during the American expansion? Record your notes below.

_____

_____

_____

HISTORY NOTEBOOK | UNIT 3 | CURATING HISTORY
Gilcrease Museum, Tulsa, Oklahoma

NATIONAL GEOGRAPHIC
L E A R N I N G

Explore Native American history and the history of the American West through a collection of art and artifacts from the Gilcrease Museum. Then record your responses to the questions below.

1. **Reading Check** Why did Thomas Gilcrease create a museum dedicated to Native American culture and the American West?

_____
_____

2. **Identify** Pick one of the artifacts shown in this lesson and use your own words to explain what that item reveals about Native American culture and the American West. Why did you pick the artifact you chose?

_____
_____
_____

3. Which artifact or artwork are you most interested in? What about it interests you?

_____
_____
_____

4. **Connect to Today** Think about Native American culture and the American West today. Imagine you are putting together a collection for the museum that would be viewed 100 years from now. What objects from today would you add to the collection? Explain your choices.

_____
_____
_____

5. **Form and Support Opinions** Some museums and some artifacts don't appeal to everyone, and that's to be expected. Would you want to visit this museum to see these objects? If so, why? If not, why not?

_____
_____
_____

6. **Make Generalizations** Based on the collection in this lesson, what generalizations can you make about the American West?

_____
_____
_____

HISTORY NOTEBOOK | UNIT **3** | **AMERICAN GALLERY**
The Trail of Tears

Driven off their lands, Native Americans were forced to march from the southeastern states to land west of the Mississippi. Thousands died in this imposed relocation, now known as the Trail of Tears.

1. **Analyze Cause and Effect** What actions led to the Trail of Tears?

_____

_____

_____

2. **Make Connections** What story about the United States do these photographs as a group tell?

_____

_____

_____

3. **Describe** For each photograph, write down three adjectives that you think describe the mood, purpose, or central idea of that photo.

_____

_____

_____

_____

4. **Evaluate** A photograph can act as a powerful tool to tell a story and evoke emotion. Which photograph do you think is the most compelling in telling the story of the Trail of Tears and what emotions does it evoke? Explain your reasoning.

_____

_____

_____

5. This American Gallery features several sculptures or sites that serve as memorials to Native Americans and the Trail of Tears. Knowing what you know now about the Trail of Tears, how would you pay homage to those forced to leave their lands? Create a memorial and write your description below. Conduct additional research if necessary.

_____

_____

_____

_____

HISTORY NOTEBOOK | UNIT **3** | AMERICAN STORY ONLINE **The Writers and Artists of Concord, Massachusetts**

NATIONAL GEOGRAPHIC LEARNING

Learn about the "genius cluster" of artists and writers in Concord, Massachusetts.

1. **Reading Check** What is transcendentalism and its core beliefs? Who were some of the key transcendentalists?

_____

_____

_____

2. **Analyze Language Use** Review Ralph Waldo Emerson's quote from his essay "Self-Reliance." What does he mean by the repeated use of the word sacred? Using your own words, explain what point you think he is making.

_____

_____

_____

3. **Draw Conclusions** What is the importance of nature to the human soul?

_____

_____

_____

4. **Discuss and Debate** Form a group with three other classmates to discuss and debate this question: Is it better to be a conformist or an individualist? Have two of you argue for being a conformist and the other two argue for being an individualist. Are there times when it's best to conform or better to rebel? Record notes for each argument below.

_____

_____

_____

5. **Form and Support Opinions** Based on what you learned, which philosophical approach do you think you take—transcendentalism or enlightenment? Explain your reasoning.

_____

_____

_____

6. You learned about several writers and artists in this American Story. Which person did you most relate to or find most interesting? Research your selected writer or artist and then create a 3-minute presentation about him or her to present to the class. Use the space below to record your notes.

_____

_____

_____

HISTORY NOTEBOOK · UNIT 3

THROUGH THE LENS, AMERICAN PLACES
Rocky Mountain National Park

NATIONAL GEOGRAPHIC
L E A R N I N G

Find out more about one of the great national parks in the United States—Rocky Mountain National Park—and see why this landscape continues to inspire artists. After reading the text, answer the questions below.

1. Reading Check How were the Rocky Mountains formed?

_____

_____

_____

2. Describe Study the photograph. What are your first impressions of photograph? In your own words, write a caption for the photograph describing what you see and what feelings the image conveys.

_____

_____

_____

3. Have you been to Rocky Mountain National Park? If so, describe what it was like when you visited. If not, have you been to other national parks? How would you describe the park you visited? If you haven't been to any national parks, would you want to visit this one? Why or why not?

_____

_____

_____

_____

4. Make Inferences Artists have long been inspired by the landscape of Rocky Mountain National Park. Why do you think artists want to capture the image of the park? And why would it be important to do so?

_____

_____

_____

5. Compare and Contrast List 5 adjectives that you would use to describe the landscape based on the photo in the lesson. Compare your list with that of one of your classmates. To what extent do you both see this place in a similar way? How did your impressions vary?

_____

_____

_____

_____

HISTORY NOTEBOOK | **UNIT 3** | **AMERICAN VOICES**
Elizabeth Cady Stanton

NATIONAL GEOGRAPHIC
L E A R N I N G

Review the American Voices lesson to learn about one of the key—and controversial—leaders in the early fight for women's rights, and then respond to the questions below.

1. Reading Check What events led to the formation of the National Woman Suffrage Association?

_____

_____

_____

2. Analyze Language Use Elizabeth Cady Stanton said, "The best protector any woman can have . . . is courage." What did she mean by that statement? Do you agree with her? Why or why not?

_____

_____

_____

_____

3. Identify How did Stanton exemplify courage? What other personal qualities and skills did she have that made her a leader in the women's movement?

_____

_____

_____

_____

4. Stanton was a remarkable person who dedicated her life fighting for women's rights. Support that statement with your own opinions about her accomplishments—or explain why you aren't all that impressed with her.

_____

_____

_____

5. Evaluate In what ways have women's rights improved since the establishment of the National American Woman Suffrage Association? Have women's rights gotten better or worse over the years? How so? How do you think Stanton would react to women's issues today?

_____

_____

_____

HISTORY NOTEBOOK | **UNIT 3** | AMERICAN GALLERY
The Hudson River School

NATIONAL GEOGRAPHIC
L E A R N I N G

Go online to study American landscapes and the great artists who created them. Record your thoughts and responses to the questions below.

1. **Identify** The Hudson River School was a mid-19th century American art movement. What is it known for and why is it significant?

_____

_____

_____

2. **Evaluate** Of the landscape paintings shown, which one do you like best? What about that painting appeals to you?

_____

_____

_____

_____

3. **Describe** Select one of the paintings shown in this gallery and study it closely. What adjectives would you use to describe it? How would you describe the mood as well as the physical landscape? Consider also the lighting, colors, and style.

_____

_____

_____

_____

4. **Explore Identity** What do the paintings of these landscapes convey about American identity? Conduct online research to find a modern painting of the American landscape in recent years. What does your selected landscape reveal about American identity now?

_____

_____

_____

5. **Compare and Contrast** Go online to find three to five paintings of American landscapes from a different time period. Compare the paintings in this gallery with those that you researched. How are their styles similar? How are their styles different?

_____

_____

_____

Use the questions below to reflect on what you learned in this American Story about Chicano history and culture.

1. **Reading Check** What events led to the Mexican-American War?

_____

_____

_____

2. **Identify** What parts of North America did Mexico control in 1821?

_____

_____

_____

3. **Make Predictions** How might the United States be different if Mexico had won the Mexican-American War?

_____

_____

_____

4. What did you find most surprising or interesting in this American Story and why?

_____

_____

_____

5. **Compare and Contrast** Describe life for Mexican settlers before and after the Mexican-American War. How did settlement patterns change before and after the war? In your own words, describe people's reasons for settling in California and Texas before and after the war.

_____

_____

_____

_____

_____

_____

_____

_____

HISTORY NOTEBOOK | UNIT 3 | THROUGH THE LENS
Michael Nichols

Look through the lens of National Geographic Photographer Michael Nichols to study the giant sequoias of California. Then reflect on your thoughts below.

1. Reading Check Why does Michael Nichols photograph the wonders of the natural world?

_____

_____

_____

2. Make Inferences Why do you think the giant sequoia in the photograph is named "the President"?

_____

_____

_____

3. Nichols is a nature photographer. Would you want to do what he does for a living? Why or why not? What aspects of his job did you find interesting or unappealing?

_____

_____

_____

4. Describe What words first come to mind when you view this photograph? List 5 adjectives you would use to describe the tree and scene. Think about the physical description as well as the mood of the photo.

_____

_____

_____

5. Turn and Talk Discuss with a partner the purpose of nature photography. Is it effective in its purpose? Why or why not? Discuss other ways to achieve the same purpose. Write your notes below.

_____

_____

_____

6. Make Connections How does this photograph of "the President" convey the relationship between the natural world and human life?

_____

_____

_____

HISTORY NOTEBOOK | UNIT 3

CURATING HISTORY
Mexic-Arte Museum

NATIONAL GEOGRAPHIC
L E A R N I N G

Study the objects from the Mexic-Arte Museum, and then answer the questions below.

1. Reading Check How does the museum achieve its mission of reaching out to young adults?

_____

_____

_____

2. Make Generalizations This collection of artifacts is focused on Mexican art and objects. What generalizations can you make about the craftsmanship and design of the objects and art?

_____

_____

_____

3. Pick one of the items shown in this collection. What details do you find most interesting about it? What other information do you want to know about your selection?

_____

_____

_____

4. Make Inferences The illustrated encyclopedia is one of thousands of rare books and print materials found at the museum. Why might the museum want to preserve so many books?

_____

_____

_____

5. Evaluate In your opinion, which artifact reveals the most about Mexican culture and why? What does it convey about the culture?

_____

_____

_____

6. Visual Literacy You can work to develop your skills of observation. Pick one of the objects in the gallery and write 3 questions you think you should be asking as you look at the item. If you know the answers to your questions, write the answers too.

_____

_____

_____

HISTORY NOTEBOOK | **UNIT 3** | *REID ON THE ROAD*
The Gold Rush

Join Robert Reid as he finds out more about the California Gold Rush at the Kennedy Gold Mine in Jackson, California.

1. **Make Inferences** Do you think life was better in California before the Gold Rush? Or was it better after the Gold Rush? Explain your answer below.

_____

_____

_____

2. **Connect to Today** Once word spread about gold found in California, thousands of people flocked to California. Would you be a "gold seeker"? If so, why? If not, why not?

_____

_____

_____

3. Doug Ketron, mining engineer at the Kennedy gold mine, explains the mining process for gold. What did you find most interesting or surprising about that process?

_____

_____

_____

_____

4. Imagine you are a reporter in 1848 reporting on the start of the Gold Rush. Write a news article about the great race to find gold. Include an interview with James W. Marshall. Record the questions you would ask below. Then write your article.

_____

_____

_____

_____

_____

_____

_____

_____

_____

HISTORY NOTEBOOK | UNIT **3** | GEOLOGY IN HISTORY **How Geology Built the Transcontinental Railroad**

NATIONAL GEOGRAPHIC L E A R N I N G

As people moved west to California, transportation needed to be developed to get people there quicker and easier. Learn how geology played a role in connecting California with the rest of the country.

1. **Reading Check** What factors did surveyors need to consider in finding possible routes for the transcontinental railroad?

_____

_____

_____

2. **Identify Problems and Solutions** What geological features created obstacles for the railroad route proposed by Theodore Judah, and what would be needed to overcome those obstacles?

_____

_____

_____

3. **Describe** How would you describe the topography of the transcontinental railroad's route?

_____

_____

_____

4. **Make Inferences** Today most people can travel across the continent in an airplane. You've learned about how geology affected railroad routes—what do you think affects flight routes? What would conditions and routes would airlines and pilots have to consider when flying across the continent? What about when flying overseas?

_____

_____

_____

5. **Turn and Talk** Form a group with two other classmates to discuss the planning of the transcontinental railroad. Imagine that two of you are planners and one person in your group is a representative from Congress. The two planners, one northerner and one southerner, come up with their own proposals for the route and then present them to the representative. Then have the representative choose which route would work best. Planners should consider the geology of their route and include a map highlighting the route.

_____

_____

_____

_____

Once that first flake of gold was discovered, the rush was on to find more gold. After viewing the photographs in this American Gallery, use the prompts below to record what you learned about the gold rush.

1. **Analyze Cause and Effect** Once gold was discovered in California, what impact did it have on the state and the nation? What technologies developed as a result of the gold rush?

_____

_____

_____

_____

2. What do you learn from these photographs that you wouldn't learn from a written description of the gold rush?

_____

_____

_____

_____

3. **Describe** As you review the photographs, what are your first impressions of what life was like during the gold rush? What adjectives would you use to describe life at that time?

_____

_____

_____

_____

4. **Ask Questions** Which photograph in the gallery do you want to learn more about? Pick one and write at least three questions you have about that photograph.

_____

_____

_____

_____

5. **Draw Conclusions** What conclusions can you draw about the success of the gold rush?

_____

_____

_____

_____

HISTORY NOTEBOOK | **UNIT 3** | UNIT WRAP-UP
Expanding the New Nation

This unit, Expanding the New Nation, details the expansion of the United States and what life was like for those migrating westward. Use the questions below to think about what you learned in Unit 3.

A. After Reading Once you've completed Unit 3, revisit the chapters to select the topic that you find most interesting.

1. What is the topic I found most interesting in this unit?

_____

2. How or why does this topic interest me?

_____

3. What are some of the most important take-aways you got from this unit?

_____

_____

4. How does this topic relate to my life, my family, my community, and my identity?

_____

_____

_____

B. Nat Turner's Complex Legacy Review the article and respond to the questions below.

5. What is the subject of the article?

_____

6. What type of legacy did Nat Turner leave?

_____

_____

_____

7. How does this article connect with the focus of the unit? Why do you think the editors of this U.S. History program selected this article for this unit?

_____

_____

_____

C. Unit Activities As you prepare for your unit inquiry and the learning framework, record any thoughts, ideas, or lingering questions below.

_____

_____

_____

 **HISTORY NOTEBOOK** Archaeology and U.S. History

 **NATIONAL GEOGRAPHIC** L E A R N I N G

Read the Archaeology and U.S. History pages in your textbook and use the questions below to think more deeply about how archaeology adds to our understanding of history.

1. **Reading Check** What is archaeology and how does it connect with history?

_____

_____

_____

_____

2. Your text says, "Archaeologists and historians are partners in preserving the human record." Why would it be important to "preserve the human record?" What information or insights would people gain from preserving history?

_____

_____

_____

_____

_____

3. **Describe** Archaeologists study human-made objects, or artifacts, and they also look at where the artifacts are found to tell a story about a place, people, or event. What artifacts would tell your story? If someone you never met walked into your home, what would they know about you from the things you have there? Write a few sentences that capture your thoughts and feelings about your life in the United States. Then identify the objects in your home that would reveal your history.

_____

_____

_____

_____

4. Archaeologists work to uncover clues about past history but they also help preserve what becomes history, as the archaeologists did when the World Trade Center towers were destroyed. What aspects of being an archaeologist do you think you might find appealing? What aspects might not appeal to you?

_____

_____

_____

 **Archaeology and U.S. History**

5. Draw Conclusions After reviewing the map, select one area and the artifacts found there that you want to know more about. Conduct online research to find out more about the archaeological site. Then, using the visuals and text on the map along with additional research, think about what the artifacts reveal about the people and the place. What conclusions can you draw about the people and the place based on the artifacts found there? What was life like for the people living there at the time?

_____

_____

_____

_____

_____

_____

_____

6. Explore Identity What do you think the artifacts and sites shown in this feature convey about our American identity?

_____

_____

_____

_____

_____

_____

_____

7. Evaluate Imagine it's 200 years from now, and identify objects from the United States today that you think would help future archaeologists understand current-day American life. Consider what archaeologist would need to know about people today, such as what we might look like, eating habits, and social behaviors. What artifacts would reveal our physical characteristics? What artifacts would reveal more about our behavior? List the objects you chose, and explain what you think they reveal about American life today.

_____

_____

_____

_____

_____

_____

_____

HISTORY NOTEBOOK | UNIT 4

AMERICAN STORY
Abraham Lincoln: The Great Emancipator

NATIONAL GEOGRAPHIC
L E A R N I N G

In this American Story, learn more about the life of Abraham Lincoln, the 16th president of the United States, and his evolving views on slavery.

1. **Reading Check** How did Abraham Lincoln initially view slavery?

_____

_____

_____

2. **Analyze Language Use** Lincoln said, "If slavery is not wrong, nothing is wrong." What did he mean by that statement?

_____

_____

_____

3. **Make Predictions** Imagine that Lincoln survived the assassination or that John Wilkes Booth was stopped before he could shoot Lincoln. Do you think his views on slavery would have changed? If so, how so? If not, why not? What do you think he would have done about slavery, if anything?

_____

_____

_____

4. **Form and Support Opinions** Based on the Constitution, Lincoln believed the federal government did not have the right to abolish slavery in the states where it existed. Do you agree with his belief? Why or why not? Should laws, such as those regarding civil rights, be up to the states or the federal government to decide? Explain your reasoning.

_____

_____

_____

5. Have you ever felt like something was wrong or been in a situation when someone was doing something you thought was wrong or unjust? How did you feel about it, and what were your views on the situation? Use the space below to journal your thoughts and reactions. Remember, this is a space to record your thoughts for your own reference.

_____

_____

_____

_____

_____

HISTORY NOTEBOOK | **UNIT 4** | **AMERICAN VOICES**
Harriet Tubman

NATIONAL GEOGRAPHIC
L E A R N I N G

Review the American Voices lesson and then record your responses to the questions below.

1. **Reading Check** What strategies did Harriet Tubman use to help enslaved people escape to freedom on the Underground Railroad?

_____

_____

_____

2. **Analyze Cause and Effect** How did Tubman's actions during the Civil War affect the Union Army's fight against the Confederates?

_____

_____

_____

_____

3. **Make Inferences** As a conductor on the Underground Railroad, Harriet Tubman rescued about 300 slaves. In her eight years as conductor, she never lost a "passenger." What does that say about her character and skills?

_____

_____

_____

_____

4. **Make Predictions** How do you think Tubman would react to civil rights today? What would she say about the rights of African Americans today?

_____

_____

_____

_____

5. **Turn and Talk** Tubman was a remarkable leader fighting for the freedom of enslaved people before and during the Civil War. Discuss with a partner your opinions about her accomplishments, the challenges she faced, and the personal qualities someone like her would need to have in order to do what she did. Support your opinions with evidence based on what you learned.

_____

_____

_____

HISTORY NOTEBOOK | **UNIT 4**

AMERICAN GALLERY
The Underground Railroad

Learn about the Underground Railroad and those who helped people escape from slavery, and answer the questions below.

1. Evaluate After viewing the photos and reading the captions, what were you most surprised to learn about the Underground Railroad? What was surprising about it?

_____

_____

_____

2. Make Inferences What do you think life was like for those escaping slavery on the Underground Railroad?

_____

_____

_____

3. Interpret Visuals Study the two paintings shown in this gallery. Based on the visuals alone, what story about the Underground Railroad do these paintings tell? Use your own words to convey their meaning.

_____

_____

_____

_____

4. Turn and Talk The Underground Railroad was a path to freedom for enslaved African Americans. At that time, they had no civil rights, and although the Constitution said that all men were created equal, enslaved African Americans were not treated as such. Discuss with a partner what you think is different now about civil rights and equality. What is the same, and what do you think needs to change?

_____

_____

_____

5. Pick one of the people featured in this American Gallery and prepare a 3-minute presentation about that person to share with the class. Go online for more information about his or her life and accomplishments. Include additional photos with your presentation. Record your notes below.

_____

_____

_____

_____

HISTORY NOTEBOOK | UNIT **4** | **AMERICAN STORY**
Naval Battles of the Civil War

Not all battles during the Civil War were fought on land. This American Story describes three key naval battles of the Civil War. Use the questions below to capture what you learned.

1. Reading Check What is an ironclad and how would you describe it?

_____

_____

_____

2. Form and Support Opinions Who do you think won the Battle of Hampton Roads? Support your opinion with evidence based on what you learned.

_____

_____

_____

3. Make Connections How was Vicksburg critical to the Civil War?

_____

_____

_____

4. Ask Questions Imagine you could interview one of the captains or sailors from one of the ships featured in this American story. What questions would you ask about his experience?

_____

_____

_____

5. Evaluate Which naval battle did you find most interesting and why?

_____

_____

_____

6. Draw Conclusions Why would historians want to study the shipwrecks of the *Monitor* and the *Virginia*? What information about the Civil War could the shipwrecks provide?

_____

_____

_____

HISTORY NOTEBOOK | UNIT **4** | THROUGH THE LENS, AMERICAN PLACES
Manassas, Virginia

Learn about the site of two historic Civil War battles and then record your responses to the questions below.

1. **Reading Check** What is the significance of the Stone House?

_____

_____

_____

2. **Evaluate** Read the caption for the photograph. How might the landscape make Manassas a strategic site for a battle? What might be some disadvantages of the site for a battle?

_____

_____

_____

_____

3. How you ever visited a historic Civil War site? Write a few sentences about your experience there. If you haven't visited one, write a few sentences about why you might or might not want to do so.

_____

_____

_____

_____

4. **Describe** Study National Geographic photographer Ken Garrett's photograph of Manassas. Describe it in terms of photographic technique, such as perspective, lighting, and mood. What makes this particular photograph compelling?

_____

_____

_____

_____

5. This American Place is focused on a historic site from the Civil War. Do some research online to come up with information and photos of another historic site from the Civil War. Be prepared to do a 3-minute presentation on the site you found. Include a description of the significant event that took place at the site.

_____

_____

_____

HISTORY NOTEBOOK | UNIT 4 | *REID ON THE ROAD* | Civil War Medicine

Watch as Digital Nomad Robert Reid discovers the reality behind Civil War medicine. Then review the questions below and record your responses and reactions.

1. Identify What was the single fact or idea related to Civil War medicine that surprised you the most?

_____

_____

_____

_____

2. As you watch the video, write down three ideas that you want to remember from the video, and explain why you think they are important.

_____

_____

_____

_____

3. Connect to Today What does the video about Civil War medicine tell you about medicine today? What practices from the Civil War are still in place today? What has changed?

_____

_____

_____

_____

4. Turn and Talk National Museum of Civil War Medicine curator Jake Wynn says, "We often look at warfare as being the driver of new revolutions and technology." Do you agree? Why or why not? Discuss with a partner and then come up with an example of another historical event that brought us new technology still in use today. Record your notes below.

_____

_____

_____

_____

5. Imagine it's 200 years from now. Identify a technology or invention from your life today that you think would help future generations. List the object you chose below and explain why you think it will still be important in the future.

_____

_____

_____

_____

HISTORY NOTEBOOK | **UNIT 4** | NATIONAL GEOGRAPHIC PHOTOGRAPHER
Sam Abell

National Geographic photographer Sam Abell knew from a young age that he wanted to be a photographer. Find out about his journey and how he brings physical environments to life with his photography.

1. **Reading Check** Why is Sam Abell considered "not the typical photographer?"

_____

_____

_____

2. **Describe** Study the photograph of the flooded Mississippi on Water Street. What is your initial reaction to the photograph? What about it do you find compelling?

_____

_____

_____

3. **Evaluate** What can photographs like Abell's tell people about American culture and geography that written descriptions might not?

_____

_____

_____

4. **Compare and Contrast** Abell follows a "compose and wait" approach to photography and his photos are described as "quiet" while another approach to photography might be more immediate and in the moment with photos that are lively and action-oriented. Conduct research to find a "lively" photo of the Mississippi River and compare it to one of Abell's photos. Which style do you prefer? What do you like about each style and what do you not like?

_____

_____

_____

_____

5. When Abell first worked for National Geographic, he thought, "This is the right place for me; this is my life." He knew he had found the place to pursue his passion. What hobby or activity are you passionate about? What do you enjoy about it, and do you want to pursue it further as a career?

_____

_____

_____

HISTORY NOTEBOOK | **UNIT 4** | *REID ON THE ROAD*
Gettysburg Re-enactors

NATIONAL GEOGRAPHIC
L E A R N I N G

Find out about the role re-enactors play in preserving American history with Digital Nomad Robert Reid. In this video, he meets with Civil War re-enactors and living historian Ed Mantell to learn about Gettysburg.

1. **Identify** What part of the video did you find most interesting? Why did you find it interesting?

_____

_____

2. What's the difference between a re-enactor and a living historian? Which would you rather be? Explain why you chose the role you did.

_____

_____

_____

3. **Form and Support Opinions** What might be appealing about being a re-enactor? What would be challenging?

_____

_____

4. Ed Mantell notes that re-enactment as a hobby has been going on at least 100 years. Why do you think re-enactments have continued over the years? How do re-enactments contribute to what we know about American history?

_____

_____

_____

5. **Ask Questions** After watching the video, what questions do you have for re-enactors and living historians?

_____

_____

_____

6. Imagine it's 200 years from now and identify a current event you think might be re-enacted in the future. Provide instructions for re-enacting the event. Consider the setting, clothing, and props needed.

_____

_____

_____

_____

_____

_____

HISTORY NOTEBOOK | **UNIT 4**

CURATING HISTORY
National Civil War Museum

NATIONAL GEOGRAPHIC
L E A R N I N G

Explore the artifacts from the National Civil War Museum, and then answer the questions below.

1. Reading Check Why would a museum want to tell the story of the Civil War without bias?

_____

_____

_____

2. Evaluate Pick one artifact shown in this lesson and use your own words to explain what that artifact reveals about the Civil War. Why did you pick the artifact you chose?

_____

_____

_____

_____

3. Identify What collection of artifacts would you put together to tell the story of the Civil War from the Union's perspective? From the Confederate's perspective?

_____

_____

_____

_____

4. Think about all the jobs or careers involved in just getting these artifacts on the page. They might include archaeologists, historians, conservators, museum curators, writers, editors, and designers. What if any of those jobs seem interesting to you? Explain which ones you might want to learn more about.

_____

_____

_____

_____

5. Form and Support Opinions Would you want to visit this museum to see these objects and other collections about the Civil War? If so, why? If not, why not?

_____

_____

_____

_____

HISTORY NOTEBOOK | UNIT 4 | AMERICAN GALLERY
The Battle of Vicksburg

Go online to view this American Gallery about one of the key battles of the Civil War and respond to the questions below.

1. **Make Inferences** How do the visuals in this American Gallery help you understand what the Battle of Vicksburg was like? What do the photos tell you about the American experience during the Civil War?

_____

_____

_____

_____

2. **Evaluate** Review the paintings showing the siege of Vicksburg. What is your reaction to the paintings? Which do you think is more powerful, a written passage about the battle or one of these paintings? Explain your reasoning.

_____

_____

_____

_____

3. **Ask and Answer Questions** As you explore the gallery, write down three questions you have about the battle of Vicksburg. Then pair up with a partner, trade questions, and try to answer your partner's questions.

_____

_____

_____

_____

4. **Describe** If you had to pick three adjectives to describe the Battle of Vicksburg based on the photographs and items in this gallery, what would those three adjectives be?

_____

_____

_____

_____

5. **Compare and Contrast** Conduct online research to find a detailed map of the Battle of Vicksburg. Compare your detailed map with the illustrated map shown in the gallery. How are the maps different? Which map is more effective and why?

_____

_____

_____

_____

Read about life in the United States after the Civil War and how the North emerged from the war. Then answer the questions below.

1. **Reading Check** How was the North's economy affected by the war?

_____

_____

_____

2. **Summarize** In what ways did Congress give the North advantages over the South?

_____

_____

_____

_____

3. **Compare and Contrast** Based on what you learned about the North after the Civil War, what do you think life was like in the South after the Civil War? What similarities did the North and South face after the war?

_____

_____

_____

_____

4. **Identify** What is the most important thing you want to remember from this story about life after the Civil War in the North?

_____

_____

_____

_____

5. **Turn and Talk** Discuss with a partner what life was like for African Americans in the North after the war. What connections can you make between the struggles of African Americans after the Civil War, during the civil rights movement, and today? Record your notes below.

_____

_____

_____

_____

HISTORY NOTEBOOK | UNIT **4**

AMERICAN GALLERY
Education, Land, and Resistance

Learn more about life after the Civil War in this American Gallery. Respond to the questions below.

1. Identify What were some of the key changes made during Reconstruction in the effort to help freedmen?

_____

_____

_____

2. Identify Problems and Solutions What were some of the challenges the freedmen faced after the Civil War? What steps did they take to overcome challenges?

_____

_____

_____

_____

3. Evaluate How do these photographs help you understand the period of Reconstruction after the Civil War?

_____

_____

_____

_____

4. Analyze Cause and Effect How was Reconstruction affected after President Lincoln's assassination? Using your own words, provide at least one example as highlighted in this gallery.

_____

_____

_____

_____

5. Review and read the Lost Friends ads in this gallery. At the time, the best way to find family and friends was through these ads. What technology would you use today to share information or reconnect with family or friends? Imagine you needed to find someone who you lost contact with. Write your own "ad" in a current-day format to reconnect with this person.

_____

_____

_____

_____

UNIT WRAP-UP
The Deepest Crisis

This unit, The Deepest Crisis, explores the divisive time before, during, and after the Civil War. Use the questions below to think about what you learned in Unit 4.

A. After Reading Once you've completed Unit 4, revisit the chapters to select the topic that you find most interesting.

1. What is the topic I found most interesting in this unit?

_____

2. How or why does this topic interest me?

_____

3. What are some of the most important take-aways you got from this unit?

_____

_____

4. How does this topic relate to my life, my family, my community, and my identity?

_____

_____

_____

B. A Sketch in Time Review the article and respond to the questions below.

5. What is the subject of the article?

_____

6. Why would be important to have artists sketch war scenes? What can they capture that a photograph might not?

_____

_____

_____

7. How does this article connect with the focus of the unit? Why do you think the editors of this U.S. History program selected this article for this unit?

_____

_____

_____

C. Unit Activities As you prepare for your unit inquiry and the learning framework, record any thoughts, ideas, or lingering questions below.

_____

_____

AMERICAN STORY
The Wild West

The Wild West in history might not be as wild as the Wild West we see in movies and television today. Learn about the real west in this American Story and why the legend of the Wild West has persisted throughout the years. Then respond to the prompts below.

1. Reading Check What was the "Real West" actually like?

_____

_____

_____

2. Describe Which movies or television shows about the Wild West have you seen? Based on what you have seen, how would you describe America's west? If you haven't watched any movies or television shows about the Wild West, write a few sentences to describe what you think the Wild West was like.

_____

_____

_____

_____

3. Make Inferences Why do you think the "larger-than-life" image of the West was created?

_____

_____

_____

4. Explore Identity What American identity did the Wild West represent? What in current popular culture represents the American identity today, and how would you describe that identity?

_____

_____

_____

_____

5. Turn and Talk Pair up with a classmate and discuss this question: *How has popular culture represented periods of time or places in history?* As you discuss the question, explain your reasoning. Be sure to identify specific examples in popular culture. Record your notes below.

_____

_____

_____

_____

HISTORY NOTEBOOK | **UNIT 5**

GEOLOGY IN HISTORY
How Geology Waters the Great Plains

Geology plays an important role in the freshwater we use every day. After reading about how geology waters the Great Plains, record your responses to the questions below.

1. **Reading Check** Describe the geology of the Great Plains and the environmental problems in the region prior to the 1950s.

_____

_____

_____

2. In your own words, explain how aquifers work.

_____

_____

_____

3. The Ogallala Aquifer is drying up through overuse. How would you go about persuading people to create rules for responsible groundwater extraction and to follow those rules once established?

_____

_____

_____

_____

4. **Ask Questions** Andrés Ruzo, a geologist and National Geographic Explorer, wrote the information in this lesson. After reading the lesson, what additional questions about geology would you want to ask him? What do you want to find out more about?

_____

_____

_____

_____

5. **Describe** How does the physical landscape of the Great Plains differ from the landscape where you live? How does your region get freshwater? Do a little research to locate the main source of freshwater in your community.

_____

_____

_____

_____

HISTORY NOTEBOOK | UNIT **5** | THROUGH THE LENS, AMERICAN PLACES
America's Breadbasket—The Great Plains

This American Place describes what is known as American's Breadbasket—the region of the Great Plains. Study the photograph, text, and caption and then respond to the questions below.

1. Reading Check Why is the Great Plains region considered the breadbasket of North America?

_____

_____

2. Describe Based on the photograph, how would you describe the Great Plains? What else would you expect to see in the Great Plains?

_____

_____

_____

3. Go online and find other photographs of the Great Plains. Create a photo gallery of the Great Plains using at least 5 images, and write captions to go with each photograph. Be prepared to present your photo gallery to the class.

_____

_____

_____

_____

_____

_____

4. Pick one of the crops grown in the Great Plains and go online to find the types of products—food and otherwise—made from this crop. Create a graphic or diagram to show the products that come from your selected crop. Sketch your diagram below.

HISTORY NOTEBOOK | **UNIT 5**

CURATING HISTORY
The Field Museum, Chicago, Illinois

NATIONAL GEOGRAPHIC
L E A R N I N G

Explore the Field Museum of Natural History in Chicago, Illinois, and then record your responses to the questions below.

1. **Reading Check** What type of museum is the Field Museum and what does it showcase?

_____

_____

2. **Form and Support Opinions** Read Associate Curator Bill Parkinson's quotation. Do you agree with his statement? Why or why not?

_____

_____

_____

3. **Identify** Pick one of the artifacts shown in this lesson and use your own words to explain what that artifact reveals about the culture. Why did you pick the artifact you chose?

_____

_____

_____

4. This collection of artifacts is focused on the Columbian Exposition and three Native American tribes. Select one of the topics and do a little research online to come up with photos of additional artifacts from either the Columbian Exposition or one of the specific tribes. Find a way to share the artifacts you found with your classmates, and be prepared to talk for 30 seconds about each one. Record your notes on the objects below.

_____

_____

_____

5. **Make Inferences** Why might it be important to collect and display Native American artifacts in a museum?

_____

_____

_____

6. Some museums and some artifacts don't appeal to everyone, and that's to be expected. Would you want to visit this museum to see these objects? If so, why? If not, why not?

_____

_____

AMERICAN GALLERY
The Battle of Little Bighorn

Go online to view this American Gallery about the Battle of Little Bighorn and respond to the questions below.

1. Evaluate Which photograph in this gallery do you find most interesting? Explain why.

_____

_____

_____

2. What did you learn about the Battle of Bighorn through this collection of photographs that you didn't already know or didn't already read about?

_____

_____

_____

3. Ask Questions Pick the photograph or painting that raised the most questions for you, and write a few of the questions you have below.

_____

_____

_____

4. Describe Select one photograph or painting to study closely. Describe the image as you would to someone unable to view it. What adjectives would you use? What mood or emotions would you try to convey?

_____

_____

_____

5. Create your own collection of images to tell the story of the Battle of Little Bighorn. Go online to find paintings, photographs, or artifacts related to the battle. Select four or five images that you think add to the story of the Battle of Little Bighorn. Write captions for each photo.

_____

_____

_____

_____

_____

_____

_____

HISTORY NOTEBOOK | **UNIT 5** | AMERICAN STORY
Working in America

Learn about industrial America and the birth of the labor movement in this American Story. Then record your thoughts on the questions below.

1. **Reading Check** What conditions led to the birth of the modern labor movement?

_____

_____

2. **Identify** In this American Story, you learned about several labor activists. What personal qualities do you think an activist would need to have? List three qualities and explain why they would be important.

_____

_____

_____

_____

3. Of the labor activists you read about, which one do you want to learn more about and why?

_____

_____

_____

_____

4. Conduct a little online research to identify a current work issue, such as the rate of minimum wage. Then write a short speech as an advocate for that work issue.

_____

_____

_____

_____

_____

5. **Form and Support Opinions** Do you think labor unions are still necessary today? Why or why not?

_____

_____

_____

_____

HISTORY NOTEBOOK **UNIT 5** CURATING HISTORY **California State Railroad Museum, Sacramento**

Take a look "inside" the California State Railroad Museum, and then answer the questions below.

1. Reading Check What are some types of exhibits found in this museum?

_____

_____

_____

2. Why would it be important to chronicle railroad history?

_____

_____

_____

3. Make Inferences What does the railroad museum and the artifacts tell you about American life?

_____

_____

_____

4. Describe The California State Railroad Museum's collection of artifacts from the railroad industry tells you about the transportation technology. What objects from today would you put together in a collection to describe current-day transportation technology? Describe the items in that collection.

_____

_____

_____

5. Think about all the jobs or careers involved in just getting these artifacts on the page. They might include archaeologists, historians, conservators, museum curators, writers, editors, and designers. What if any of those jobs seem interesting to you? Explain which ones you might want to learn more about.

_____

_____

_____

6. Identify If you were to visit this museum, based on the artifacts you see in this lesson, what other kinds of objects would you expect to find in this same exhibit?

_____

_____

_____

HISTORY NOTEBOOK | UNIT **5** | *REID ON THE ROAD*
Angel Island

Most people know about Ellis Island, the place where millions of immigrants passed through to reach the United States. But immigrants also came to another place: Angel Island. Join Digital Nomad Robert Reid to learn about Angel Island and its stories. After watching the video, record your thoughts on the questions below.

1. **Identify** As you watch the video, write down three ideas that you want to remember from the video, and explain why you think they are important.

_____

_____

_____

2. **Turn and Talk** Discuss with a partner what life might have been like for a Chinese immigrant at Angel Island. Then discuss what you know about Ellis Island and the immigration process there to compare the two locations. Write your notes below.

_____

_____

_____

3. Interview an immigrant to find out his or her story. Find someone who immigrated to the United States, either someone you know, a family member, or even someone who has a relative who immigrated in the past. Prepare at least three questions, conduct your interview, and write your interviewee's story below.

_____

_____

_____

_____

4. **Form and Support Opinions** The park ranger Robert Reid meets with says that current stories about immigration are the same as the stories that happened 100 years ago at Angel Island. Do you agree with him? Why or why not? Find a current immigration story or article, either online or in print. Then compare that story with the stories in the video. Record your observations below.

_____

_____

_____

5. In what ways have people's attitudes toward immigrants changed since Angel Island? Have attitudes gotten better or worse over the years? Explain your answer.

_____

_____

_____

HISTORY NOTEBOOK | **UNIT 5**

THROUGH THE LENS
Immigration

NATIONAL GEOGRAPHIC
L E A R N I N G

Study the photographs in this Through the Lens look at immigration, and then record your thoughts using the prompts below.

1. **Reading Check** How did New York City's population and demographics change between 1870 and 1915?

_____

_____

2. **Evaluate** How do the photographs help you understand the history of immigration? What story do these photos tell you about immigrant experience in the United States?

_____

_____

_____

_____

3. **Form and Support Opinions** Do you agree with President Kennedy's statement that we are a "nation of immigrants"? Why or why not?

_____

_____

_____

_____

4. In this lesson, the question is asked, *How is immigration a piece of your American story?* Tell your immigration story or interview someone else for his or her immigration story.

_____

_____

_____

_____

5. Select one photo that you find most interesting. What is most interesting to you about it? Then write what you think might be the story behind the photograph. Write your notes below or sketch out a storyboard.

_____

_____

_____

_____

Name _____

Jane Addams was a pioneer activist and social worker in the United States during the late 1800s and early 1900s. After reading about her work and life, take time to record your thoughts below.

---

1. **Reading Check** How did Hull House help the Chicago community?

_____

_____

---

2. **Analyze Language Use** Read Harold Ickes quotation about Jane Addams. What do you think he means when he calls her the "truest American"?

_____

_____

3. Jane Addams was a remarkable person who dedicated her life to helping others. Support that statement with your own opinions about her accomplishments—or explain why you aren't all that impressed with her.

_____

_____

_____

4. **Make Generalizations** Do you see Addams as a role model? Is she someone you would try to emulate? If so, why? If not, why not?

_____

_____

_____

5. **Identify** What personal qualities do you think a person who does what Jane Addams did would need to have? List three qualities and explain why they would be important.

_____

_____

_____

_____

6. **Make Inferences** What advice do you think Addams would give you and your classmates if she were still alive? How do you think she would react to American life today?

_____

_____

_____

_____

Name

HISTORY NOTEBOOK | UNIT 5 | AMERICAN GALLERY
The Age of Invention

Study the photographs in this American Gallery to learn about some of the most significant inventions in U.S. history. Then respond to the prompts below.

1. **Compare and Contrast** Review the photos and captions for Berliner's gramophone and Edison's phonograph. How are they similar, and what is different about them? What device is used today to record sound? What is the same and what is different about today's device?

_____

_____

2. **Explore Identity** What do you think these inventions—and these inventors—convey about the American identity?

_____

_____

_____

3. **Evaluate** Of the inventions shown in this gallery, which one do you think is the greatest invention and why?

_____

_____

_____

4. Of the inventors featured in this gallery, who are you most interested in and why? Go online to find out more about this person and create a social media profile for the inventor you selected.

_____

_____

_____

5. **Draw Conclusions** What conclusions can you draw about the role of the Age of Invention and the innovations featured in this gallery in the American experience today?

_____

_____

_____

6. Imagine it's 200 years from now, and identify an invention from your life today that you think is one of the greatest inventions in modern society. Think about how it would help future generations understand American life. List the invention you chose below. Explain its significance and what you think it reveals about American life today.

_____

_____

_____

HISTORY NOTEBOOK | UNIT **5** | AMERICAN STORY
The Triangle Waist Company Factory Fire

NATIONAL GEOGRAPHIC
L E A R N I N G

In 1911, an event took place that forever changed the labor laws in the United States. The Triangle Waist Company factory fire was a tragic event that could've been prevented. Read about how the event unfolded and the aftermath in this American Story.

1. Reading Check What set of conditions could have prevented the tragedy of the factory fire?

_____

_____

_____

2. Make Inferences How do you think company owners would react to employee grievances after this event?

_____

_____

_____

3. Evaluate This American Story features many quotes from those who experienced the fire. What do you learn from the quotes about the event that you wouldn't learn from a written description of the event?

_____

_____

_____

4. Ask Questions If you were to interview a female garment worker, what questions would you ask? List your questions below. How do you think she would answer the questions?

_____

_____

_____

5. Connect to Today In news accounts, find either a recent workplace disaster or a workplace issue, such as poor working conditions, from anywhere around the world. Take notes about how that event or issue affected local people and how the international community responded. How would you resolve the issue or prevent further disasters? What steps do you think can be taken? Write your thoughts below.

_____

_____

_____

_____

_____

HISTORY NOTEBOOK | UNIT 5

THROUGH THE LENS, AMERICAN PLACES

The Grand Canyon, Northwestern Arizona

NATIONAL GEOGRAPHIC
L E A R N I N G

Read the introductory text, quote, and caption for the photograph in this feature. Then respond to the questions below.

1. **Reading Check** How did President Theodore Roosevelt protect the Grand Canyon?

_____

_____

2. Have you been to the Grand Canyon? If so, describe what it was like when you visited. If not, explain why you might or might not want to go.

_____

_____

3. **Interpret Maps** Use a map in your textbook or a classroom map to locate this American Place. Figure out roughly how far this place is from where you live. How do the geography and topography of this place differ from where you live?

_____

_____

4. **Describe** List 5 adjectives that you would use to describe this place based on the photo in the lesson. Compare your list with that of one of your classmates. To what extent do you both see this place in a similar way? How did your impressions vary?

_____

_____

_____

5. **Form and Support Opinions** As tourism grows, commercial groups have wanted to build along the canyon edge. Review President Roosevelt's quote. Do you think that the Grand Canyon should be protected or that development should be allowed to accommodate tourists? Explain your reasoning.

_____

_____

_____

6. Go online to find other images of the Grand Canyon. Find at least four different photographs, and then prepare a two-minute presentation to describe the Grand Canyon and what it says about the American identity. Record your notes below, and be prepared to share your presentation with the class.

_____

_____

_____

HISTORY NOTEBOOK UNIT **5**

AMERICAN GALLERY
New York City at the Turn of the Century

NATIONAL GEOGRAPHIC
L E A R N I N G

Learn about how the "greatest city in the world"—New York City—was built in this American Gallery. After reviewing the photographs, answer the questions below.

1. **Evaluate** Which photograph did you find the most interesting and why? What facts in this gallery were you most surprised to find out and why?

_____

_____

_____

_____

2. Use your own words to explain what these photographs as a group reveal about the American experience.

_____

_____

_____

_____

3. **Explore Identity** Which photograph best represents "the greatest city in the world"? Explain why you think the photo you chose best shows New York City's identity.

_____

_____

_____

_____

4. This gallery tells a story about how the city of New York was built. Think about your city or town and the story of how it was built. Find out how your community started, what buildings or areas were built, and any other information you think helps tell the story of your town. What collection of photographs would you put together as a gallery about your community? Record your ideas below, and then write a brief caption for each photo you would use.

_____

_____

_____

_____

_____

_____

HISTORY NOTEBOOK | **UNIT 5** | **UNIT WRAP-UP**
Growth and Reform

This unit, Growth and Reform, focuses on rapid urban growth and the influx of immigrants—and the challenges that come with that increasing growth. Use the questions below to think about what you learned in Unit 5.

A. After Reading Once you've completed Unit 5, revisit the chapters to select the topic that you find most interesting.

1. What is the topic I found most interesting in this unit?

_____

2. How or why does this topic interest me?

_____

3. What are some of the most important take-aways I got from this unit?

_____

_____

4. How does this topic relate to my life, my family, my community, and my identity?

_____

_____

B. Nature for Everyone Review the article and respond to the questions below.

5. What is the subject of the article?

_____

6. What are some ways National Geographic Explorer Nalini Nadkarni is "bringing nature to everyone?"

_____

_____

7. How does this article connect with the focus of the unit? Why do you think the editors of this U.S. History program selected this article for this unit?

_____

_____

_____

C. Unit Activities As you prepare for your unit inquiry and the learning framework, record any thoughts, ideas, or lingering questions below.

_____

_____

_____

_____

Name

HISTORY NOTEBOOK | UNIT **6** | AMERICAN STORY
The Sinking of the Lusitania

NATIONAL GEOGRAPHIC LEARNING

In 1915, the United States had stayed away from World War I. But one event was about to change that—the sinking of the RMS Lusitania, a British passenger liner. This American Story recalls the attack on the Lusitania by a German submarine, the first in a series of events leading the United States into the war.

1. Reading Check What reason would Germany have to attack a passenger ship?

_____

_____

2. If you had booked passage on the *Lusitania* and you read the German embassy's ad that morning of your trip, would you still have gone on the ship? Explain your answer.

_____

_____

_____

3. Form and Support Opinions Although the attack was on a passenger ship and 129 Americans lost their lives, President Wilson and most Americans opposed the idea of entering the war. Do you think that the United States should have entered into the war after the sinking of the *Lusitania*? Why or why not?

_____

_____

_____

4. Pair up with a classmate to discuss different perspectives about the event. One of you takes on the perspective of a survivor, and the other takes on the perspective of the captain or another officer on the German U-boat that sunk the *Lusitania*. Describe what the event might have been like from your selected perspective. Record your notes below, and then switch roles. What new information did you learn from each perspective that you might not have considered before doing this exercise?

_____

_____

_____

_____

5. Draw Conclusions Based on what you have read and the clues left behind, do you think there was a second explosion on the ship? If so, what do you think caused the explosion? If not, explain why you don't think there was another blast. Support your response with evidence from the text.

_____

_____

_____

_____

© National Geographic Learning, a Cengage Company

HISTORY NOTEBOOK | **UNIT 6** | **THROUGH THE LENS**
Jeffrey Gusky

Read about National Geographic photographer Jeffrey Gusky and study his detailed photographs of World War I stone carvings shown in this Through the Lens feature. Explore your understanding using the prompts below.

1. **Reading Check** Why did the soldiers create the carvings?

   _____

   _____

2. **Evaluate** What more do you learn from the carvings about the soldiers and their experiences in World War I than you would from written text?

   _____

   _____

   _____

3. **Make Inferences** What do you think life was like for the soldiers living in the underground quarries?

   _____

   _____

   _____

4. National Geographic photographer Jeffrey Gusky explored underground quarries to capture these carvings and relief sculptures. What aspects of being a photographer do you think you might find appealing? What aspects might not be appealing for you?

   _____

   _____

   _____

5. **Ask Questions** Imagine you had the opportunity to interview Jeffrey Gusky. What questions would you ask him? What more do you want to know about his work? Write three to four questions below.

   _____

   _____

   _____

6. **Analyze Visuals** Pick one of the photos shown in this lesson and talk about it in terms of photographic technique. For example, is it a close-up or taken from a distance? Is there a certain angle that the photographer took that makes the photo special? What makes this particular photograph compelling or surprising?

   _____

   _____

   _____

AMERICAN GALLERY Selling World War I at Home

Go online to view this American Gallery and respond to the questions below.

1. **Evaluate** Study all the posters in this gallery. Which one is the most effective or persuasive and why? Which one is your favorite? Explain why.

_____

_____

_____

2. **Analyze Language Use** Study the stenographer's poster. What mood and tone is the poster trying to convey? What words or phrases create that tone?

_____

_____

_____

3. **Describe** Choose one of the posters and describe it as you would to someone unable to view it. What adjectives would you use? What emotions from the poster would you try to convey?

_____

_____

_____

4. **Identify** After reviewing all the posters and reading the captions, what are the key elements to advertising campaigns?

_____

_____

_____

5. What common theme or message do you notice in this American Gallery?

_____

_____

6. **Connect to Today** Think about an issue or cause in the country today that matters to you, and then create a recruitment or propaganda poster for it. If needed, conduct research online or using additional print materials. How would you promote your cause? What would you include on your poster and what would it say? Remember to include eye-catching art, compelling text, and a call to action.

_____

_____

_____

_____

HISTORY NOTEBOOK **UNIT 6** AMERICAN STORY
All that Jazz

NATIONAL GEOGRAPHIC
L E A R N I N G

Read about the birth of jazz and the blues. Use the prompts below to reflect on what you have learned.

1. Reading Check How was the blues similar to and different from jazz?

_____

_____

_____

2. Explore Identity How does jazz define the American identity? What music today do you think represents American identity? Explain your reasoning.

_____

_____

3. Identify Jazz music created the Jazz Age, influencing social trends, fashion, and dance. What popular music today influences social and cultural trends? Identify the type of music and the social trends that developed from it.

_____

_____

4. The chart on the last page shows how various types of music evolved from jazz and the blues. Modern musicians are often influenced by the great jazz and blues legends. Choose a current artist and do some research to trace the influences of that artist. Record your notes below. Listen to a few songs by that artist. Can you recognize the influence of other genres or artists? Explain.

_____

_____

5. What genre of music do you listen to most? List some of your favorite songs and explain what you like best about the music. How do you feel when you listen to the lyrics and the music?

_____

_____

_____

6. Compare and Contrast Pair up with a classmate and listen to a selected piece of jazz music or the blues. Individually, write a music review of the song and artist you listened to. Then share your reviews with each other and discuss what you liked about it and what you didn't like about it to compare perspectives.

_____

_____

_____

Name _____

Learn how geology played an important role in the 1920s and then record your responses
to the questions below.

1. Reading Check How are caves formed?

_____

_____

2. What one fact or idea were you most surprised to learn about in this lesson and why?

_____

_____

3. Describe List 5 adjectives that you would use to describe a speakeasy based on the photos in the lesson.
Compare your list with that of one of your classmates. To what extent do you both see this place in a similar
way? How did your impressions vary?

_____

_____

_____

4. Make Generalizations In what ways did geology play a part in American culture of the 1920s? What role
does geology play in today's culture?

_____

_____

_____

5. Imagine if you had to create a secluded, safe, and comfortable space for a private—but legal—event.
Where would you create this space and why? How would you tell people about the event and what
would you call it? Write or draw your plan below.

_____

_____

_____

_____

_____

_____

_____

_____

HISTORY NOTEBOOK | **UNIT 6**

REID ON THE ROAD
The Model T

NATIONAL GEOGRAPHIC
L E A R N I N G

Join Digital Nomad Robert Reid as he travels to Michigan to look for the "greatest car ever." Then use the space below to record what you learned.

1. **Identify** Who created the first automobile? Why was Henry Ford so famous?

_____

_____

_____

2. **Describe** How did Henry Ford change conditions for factory workers?

_____

_____

_____

3. Digital Nomad Robert Reid goes in search of the "greatest car ever." What do you think is the greatest car ever and why? What about it makes it great?

_____

_____

_____

4. **Form and Support Opinions** Reid says that the Model T "created" the middle class. Do you agree with that statement? Why or why not? What objects do you think represent middle-class America today?

_____

_____

_____

5. **Explore Identity** What did automobiles and the auto industry convey about the American identity? How would you describe the identity of the automobile industry today?

_____

_____

_____

6. What part of the video did you find most interesting? Why did you find it interesting?

_____

_____

_____

_____

HISTORY NOTEBOOK | **UNIT 6** | *REID ON THE ROAD*
This Is Jazz

Follow Digital Nomad Robert Reid to New Orleans, Louisiana, to find out about the birth of jazz music and discover the only national park devoted to music. Using the spaces below, write your thoughts after viewing the video.

1. **Summarize** How did New Orleans become the birthplace of jazz music?

_____

_____

_____

2. **Describe** Find a short clip of jazz music by one of the musicians noted in the video and listen to it. How would you describe jazz? Then pair up with a partner to compare your descriptions of jazz music. How did your impressions of jazz vary?

_____

_____

_____

3. **Make Inferences** The Jazz National Historic Park is the only park in the National Park Services dedicated to music. Why would a national park be created for music, and why is it the only one?

_____

_____

_____

4. What other type of music should be part of a national park? Write a brief proposal below outlining the type of music park you think should be created and why, the location of the park, what the park would look like, and the services it would provide.

_____

_____

_____

_____

_____

_____

5. **Evaluate** Robert Reid says that jazz is noted for its "attitude." What attitude do you think jazz conveys? How does that compare with music styles today? Pick a current music style and explain the type of attitude it reflects and why.

_____

_____

_____

HISTORY NOTEBOOK | **UNIT 6** | **AMERICAN VOICES**
Langston Hughes

Langston Hughes was one of the great American poets. Review the American Voices lesson and then record your responses to the questions below.

1. **Reading Check** What problems did Langston Hughes encounter after the publication of his first book of poetry?

_____

_____

2. **Make Inferences** Why do you think Hughes was referred to as "the voice of Harlem?"

_____

_____

_____

3. **Ask and Answer Questions** What question would you most like to ask Hughes if you met him right now? And how do you imagine he'd answer?

_____

_____

_____

4. What personal qualities or skills do you think a writer and poet would need to have? List three qualities and explain why they would be important.

_____

_____

_____

5. **Explore Identity** In what ways did Hughes portray the African-American identity during the Harlem Renaissance? What do you think Langston Hughes would think of the African-American identity today?

_____

_____

_____

6. Find and read the full version of Hughes' poem, "I, Too." What do you think of the poem? How does it make you feel?

_____

_____

_____

HISTORY NOTEBOOK | UNIT 6 | AMERICAN GALLERY
Going to the Movies

Going to the movies has long been one of America's favorite forms of entertainment. From silent movies in the early 1900s to the blockbuster action films we see today, movies continue to inspire, educate, and entertain us.

1. **Draw Conclusions** Why do you think movies are such a popular form of entertainment? And what do you think makes a good movie?

_____

_____

_____

2. Review the photographs from movie scenes. Based on the photographs, which movie do you think you'd want to see? What interests you about that scene?

_____

_____

_____

3. **Compare and Contrast** Review the photo of the movie palace interior. What is different about theaters today? What is the same?

_____

_____

_____

4. You learned about several actors and actresses from the 1920s and 1930s. Pick one of the film stars featured in this gallery and create a social media tweet or post to promote his or her movie. Write it from the perspective of your selected actor or actress.

_____

_____

_____

5. **Connect to Today** This gallery features some of the top actors and actresses and key films of the era. Who do you think are the top actors and actresses today? What are the most significant movies today? Create your own photo gallery of the top actors, actresses, and films in modern society. Select at least 5 photographs to feature in your gallery, and write captions for each photo.

_____

_____

_____

_____

_____

AMERICAN STORY
The Dust Bowl

Learn about one of the worst environmental disasters in the United States and its effects on the country. After reading this American Story, record your thoughts on the questions below.

1. **Reading Check** Identify the conditions that led to the Dust Bowl.

_____

_____

_____

_____

2. How would you tell the story of the Dust Bowl? Do some online research to find photographs, illustrations, or other visuals from the event. Create a visual story of the Dust Bowl using the images you select. Think about the aspects you would focus on—what do you think is most important to tell about the Dust Bowl? Record your notes below, and then share your visual story with the class.

_____

_____

_____

_____

_____

3. **Identify** The government asked photographers to document the plight of the people during the Dust Bowl. What current issue would you document so that people knew more about it? How would you document the issue? List the issue and your plan below.

_____

_____

_____

_____

_____

4. **Turn and Talk** Pair up with a classmate and discuss this question: _Do you think new technologies have a positive influence or a negative influence on communities?_ As you discuss the question, explain your reasoning. Be sure to discuss the advantages and disadvantages. Record your notes below.

_____

_____

_____

_____

_____

Read about National Geographic photographer Jimmy Chin's work and study the photograph of the 1 World Trade Center in this Through the Lens feature. Respond to the prompts below.

1. **Reading Check** What did National Geographic photographer Jimmy Chin want to capture with this photograph?

_____

_____

2. **Describe** There is a saying that "A picture is worth a thousand words." How would you describe this photograph? What story do you think the photograph tells?

_____

_____

_____

_____

3. New York City is a city of skyscrapers. Pick another city—or your own—and think about the landscape that makes up your selected city. What would you photograph to tell the story of your selected city?

_____

_____

_____

_____

4. **Ask Questions** Imagine you had the opportunity to interview Jimmy Chin. What questions would you ask him? What more do you want to know about his work? Write three to four questions below.

_____

_____

_____

_____

5. **Turn and Talk** Study the photograph and then discuss the photographic technique with a partner. For example, is it a close-up or taken from a distance? Is there a certain angle that Jimmy Chin took that makes the photo special? Why do you think he chose this angle? What makes this particular photograph compelling or surprising?

_____

_____

_____

HISTORY NOTEBOOK | **UNIT 6** | **AMERICAN GALLERY**
The Great Depression

When the stock market crashed in October 1929 that marked the beginning of the worst economic crisis in United States history. The Great Depression left millions of Americans unemployed—many of them homeless and hungry—and almost half the banks in the country devastated.

1. **Make Inferences** How do the photographs in this American Gallery help you understand what the Great Depression was like? What do the photos tell you about the American experience during the depression?

_____

_____

_____

_____

2. Which photograph do you find most interesting or compelling and why?

_____

_____

_____

_____

3. **Evaluate** Review the photo of the breadline. What is your reaction to the photo? Which do you think is more powerful, a written passage about the breadlines or a photograph about the same thing? Explain why.

_____

_____

_____

_____

4. **Describe** Choose one of the photographs and describe what a day in the life of someone hit by the Great Depression might have been like.

_____

_____

_____

_____

5. **Turn and Talk** Discuss with a partner what life might have been like during the Great Depression. How would you describe the photographs? Why do you think it was important to document the Great Depression with photography? Record your notes below.

_____

_____

_____

HISTORY NOTEBOOK | UNIT 6

AMERICAN STORY
America's Favorite Pastime

Baseball has long been considered the all-American sport. Use the questions below to think about what you learned in this American Story about baseball.

1. **Reading Check** How did the growth of radio and television impact baseball, and what role did these technologies have on sports?

_____

_____

_____

2. **Evaluate** Review the firsthand quotations from writers, journalists, and players. What do you learn from the personal quotations that you might not learn from a written description about baseball?

_____

_____

_____

3. You've read about several baseball legends. Which one do you want to know more about? Do some online research to find out more about a past baseball legend and write a few sentences about the player. What qualities do you think made this person a baseball legend?

_____

_____

_____

_____

_____

_____

4. **Explore Identity** How do you think baseball symbolizes the American identity? Do you think other sports better represent American identity? If so, which one and how does it reflect American identity? If not, why not?

_____

_____

_____

_____

_____

_____

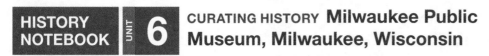

Study the objects, photographs, and captions in this Curating History lesson. Then respond to the questions below.

1. **Reading Check** What is one of the museum's key collections and why is it significant?

_____

_____

_____

_____

2. **Identify** What type of collections and objects would you expect to see in a natural and human history museum?

_____

_____

_____

_____

3. In your own words, explain why it might be important to display objects from the Milwaukee Handicraft project in a museum.

_____

_____

_____

_____

4. This museum contains a collection specific to a Milwaukee city project. Think about your city or town. What items would you include about your city or town's natural and human history? What would you want people viewing your collection to know about your city or town?

_____

_____

_____

_____

5. **Form and Support Opinions** Some museums and some artifacts don't appeal to everyone, and that's to be expected. Would you want to visit this museum to see these objects? If so, why? If not, why not?

_____

_____

_____

HISTORY NOTEBOOK | UNIT **6** | **THROUGH THE LENS, AMERICAN PLACES**
Golden Gate Bridge, San Francisco, California

Learn about the Golden Gate Bridge in San Francisco, California, and then answer the questions below.

1. **Reading Check** How did the Golden Gate Bridge impact local unions during the Great Depression?

_____

_____

2. Given what you've learned about the Golden Gate Bridge, would you have wanted to work on the bridge? Why or why not?

_____

_____

_____

3. **Describe** Have you ever been to San Francisco? How would you describe the city to someone who hasn't been there? If you haven't been to San Francisco, what do you want to know about the city from someone who has been there?

_____

_____

_____

4. **Compare and Contrast** List 5 adjectives that describe the Golden Gate Bridge and the city based on the photo in the lesson. Compare your list with that of one of your classmates. To what extent do you both see this place in a similar way? How did your impressions vary?

_____

_____

_____

5. **Make Inferences** How does the Golden Gate Bridge help you understand what it's like to live in the United States? What does it tell you about the American experience?

_____

_____

_____

6. Based on the photograph and text in the lesson, what do you find most interesting about the Golden Gate Bridge?

_____

_____

Name _____

The Federal Art Project was the visual arts arm of the Works Progress Administration. The project employed thousands of artists with a wide range of styles. The Farm Security Administration hired photographers to document rural poverty in order to convince Congress to help the poor. Both programs produced extraordinary collections of American life.

1. **Make Connections** Which photograph or painting do you think best conveys the goals of the FSA and of the FAP? Explain why.

_____

_____

2. Choose one of the photos from the gallery, and then choose one of the people featured in the photo. Speculate about what may have been going through the mind of the original person, and what may be going through the mind of the photographer at that moment.

_____

_____

3. **Make Inferences** Review Walker Evans' photograph of the flood refugees. What did Evans mean when he said he wanted his work to be "literate, authoritative, and transcendent"? Do you agree that he achieves those qualities in this photograph? Why or why not?

_____

_____

4. **Analyze Visuals** Photography is an art form all to its own. Select one of the photos to analyze, based on perspective, lighting, mood, and any other photographic techniques. How was the photo framed? What makes this particular photograph compelling?

_____

_____

_____

5. **Explore Identity** The painting by Thomas Hart Benton is one part of a series of murals. He is known for depicting the American working class and rural and small-town life with collage-like compositions that tell one big story. What does the scene shown here say about the American identity? Think about how the American identity changed. Create your own collage to show the story of the American people today. Find images online, use your own photos, clip photos from old magazines, or sketch or paint visuals to create a collage that tells your story. Record your notes below.

_____

_____

_____

_____

HISTORY NOTEBOOK | UNIT **6** | UNIT WRAP-UP
From the Great War to the New Deal

This unit, From the Great War to the New Deal, describes life during the Progressive era leading up to World War I, the prosperity of the Roaring Twenties, and the downturn of the U.S. economy during the Great Depression. Use the questions below to think about what you learned in Unit 6.

A. After Reading Once you've completed Unit 6, revisit the chapters to select the topic that you find most interesting.

1. What is the topic I found most interesting in this unit?

_____

2. How or why does this topic interest me?

_____

3. What are some of the most important take-aways I got from this unit?

_____

_____

4. How does this topic relate to my life, my family, my community, and my identity?

_____

_____

_____

B. The Hidden World of the Great War Review the article and respond to the questions below.

3. What is the subject of the article?

_____

4. What was life like in the quarries and caverns of the "underground war"?

_____

_____

5. How does this article connect with the focus of the unit? Why do you think the editors of this U.S. History program selected this article for this unit?

_____

_____

C. Unit Activities As you prepare for your unit inquiry and the learning framework, record any thoughts, ideas, or lingering questions below.

_____

_____

HISTORY NOTEBOOK UNIT 7

AMERICAN STORY ONLINE
Combat Artists of World War II

NATIONAL GEOGRAPHIC
L E A R N I N G

Using film and photographs, newsreels and newspapers brought World War II into the homes of the American public. Despite this vast coverage, the military commissioned artists to paint scenes of the war. After reading about the combat artists of World War II, review the questions below and record your thoughts.

1. **Reading Check** What were the advantages of having a combat artist paint scenes from the war?

_____

_____

2. Review Brigadier General Robert L. Denig's first quotation. Why did he think art was important during the war?

_____

_____

3. **Form and Support Opinions** After viewing both photographs and paintings of historic events, such as World War II, which medium do you think is most effective in documenting the war? Why?

_____

_____

_____

4. You read about several combat artists and reviewed their work. Choose one of the artists featured in this American Story and conduct online research to find other works made by your selected artist. Prepare a 2-minute presentation of the artist's work and explain why you selected this artist. Be sure to include the artist's bio, what you like about his work, and information about each painting.

_____

_____

_____

_____

5. Think about a historic event you studied so far. How would you document that event? What would you want to say about that moment in history? Use the space below to draw a scene from the event, highlighting it from your perspective. If needed, use additional sources to do more research.

HISTORY NOTEBOOK | UNIT **7**

AMERICAN GALLERY
The Battle of Britain

Go online to study the photographs about children and World War II in Britain in this American Gallery, and then answer the questions below.

1. **Evaluate** What do you learn from a photograph of life in Britain during the war that you wouldn't learn from a written description of the same scene or event?

_____

_____

_____

2. Which photograph do you find most interesting, and what do you find interesting about it?

_____

_____

_____

3. **Draw Conclusions** What conclusions can you draw about life for children during World War II in Britain?

_____

_____

_____

4. **Turn and Talk** During the war, many children were separated from their families and sent away from London for their safety. Do you think the children should have been sent away from their families? Discuss with a partner the pros and cons of evacuating children from the city during wartime.

_____

_____

_____

5. **Describe** Looking at the photographs as a whole, think about the overall story they tell. Describe the story as you would to someone who hasn't viewed this gallery. What details would you describe? What adjectives would you use? What emotions from the photographs would you try to convey?

_____

_____

_____

_____

HISTORY NOTEBOOK | **UNIT 7** | AMERICAN STORY
The Code Talkers of World War II

NATIONAL GEOGRAPHIC
L E A R N I N G

This American Story reveals the contributions of Navajo soldiers during World War II. Review the questions below and record your responses.

1. **Reading Check** Who were the Code Talkers, and what was their role in World War II?

_____

_____

_____

2. **Make Predictions** How might the course of World War II be different if the Navajo code project was never used?

_____

_____

_____

3. **Ask and Answer Questions** The Navajo Code Talkers were part of a group that experienced discrimination by the government yet were asked to serve their country, and did. What questions would you want to ask one of the Code Talkers about this experience? Write your questions below, and then pair up with a classmate to ask the questions, with your classmate answering as he or she thinks the soldier would've answered. Then switch roles and answer the questions your partner wrote.

_____

_____

_____

4. **Form and Support Opinions** When the Code Talkers returned home after the war, they could not talk about their work since it was classified. They endured discrimination, and they went without any recognition for their role in World War II. After many decades, the United States finally acknowledged the Code Talkers' contributions. Do you think the later efforts to recognize their work were sufficient? Why or why not? What other ideas do you have to address the treatment the Code Talkers experienced?

_____

_____

_____

5. World War II saw advancements in technology such as encryption and coding. Why do you think technologies are developed during times of war? List examples of other technologies created during wartime, noting why they were developed and how those technologies have helped or harmed society.

_____

_____

_____

_____

HISTORY NOTEBOOK | UNIT **7**

AMERICAN VOICES
Rosie the Riveter

NATIONAL GEOGRAPHIC
L E A R N I N G

Rosie the Riveter wasn't just one woman—she represented all woman who worked during World War II in the aircraft and munitions industries. Study the lesson and explore your understanding using the prompts below.

1. **Reading Check** Who was Rosie the Riveter, and how did she get her start?

_____

_____

_____

2. **Make Inferences** Why do you think the women were so good at doing their jobs? What motivated them to get the work done so quickly?

_____

_____

_____

3. **Explore Identity** Rosie the Riveter became the name and face of many women workers. What values and qualities did she reflect? How did she represent the American identity?

_____

_____

_____

4. **Connect to Today** Think about women in the workforce today and the issues they face. What symbol would you use to represent women in the workforce or the women's movement now? What title or slogan would you use? Write the description or draw the symbol that you think best reflects the women's movement today. Don't forget to include a title, name, or slogan for your symbol.

_____

_____

_____

_____

_____

_____

_____

_____

HISTORY NOTEBOOK | **UNIT 7** | *REID ON THE ROAD*
Rosie the Riveter

Rosie the Riveter is a famous American icon. Join National Geographic Digital Nomad Robert Reid as he uncovers just who Rosie was and the history behind her.

1. Identify What is a rivet and what is it used for?

_____

_____

2. Evaluate As you watch the video, write down three ideas that you want to remember from the video, and explain why you think they are important. What did you learn from this video that you didn't learn from the text lesson about Rosie the Riveter?

_____

_____

_____

3. Describe Review the Norman Rockwell poster of Rosie the Riveter and the "We Can Do it!" poster. What words would you use to describe Rosie the Riveter in those images? Do you agree that the images depict a strong image? Why or why not?

_____

_____

_____

4. Do you think you'd want to do the job that Rosie the Riveter did? What appeals to you—or not—about the job?

_____

_____

_____

5. Make Inferences In your own words, why do you think the "We Can Do It!" image of Rosie is still relevant today?

_____

_____

_____

6. In the video, you saw several posters or advertisements encouraging women to work. Imagine you needed to create a campaign asking women to work during World War II. How would you do that? Write your notes below and create a poster for your campaign. Be prepared to share it with the class.

_____

_____

_____

HISTORY NOTEBOOK **UNIT 7** CURATING HISTORY **Japanese American National Museum, Los Angeles**

Examine art from the Japanese American National Museum in Los Angeles, California, and then respond to the prompts below.

1. Reading Check What is the goal of the Japanese American National Museum?

_____

_____

2. The person who chooses and arranges the objects on display in an exhibition is called a **curator**. A curator puts these collections together to tell a story. Use your own words to describe the story this collection reveals about the experiences of Japanese Americans. What piece would you add to the art shown in this lesson to tell more about their experiences? What does that piece add to the story?

_____

_____

3. How does what you learn from the painting, sketches, and photograph change or reinforce your understanding of the internment camps?

_____

_____

4. Describe Which piece of art shown are you most interested in? What about it interests you? Select one and write a caption or story to describe the scene and the story behind the artwork.

_____

_____

_____

5. Make Inferences Why would letters written by children in the camps be of interest to the public? Why would it be important for the museum to share the letters?

_____

_____

_____

6. Each artifact in the Japanese American National Museum tells a story about the culture, history, and experiences of Japanese Americans. What story would you want to tell about your culture and experiences? Imagine if artifacts from your life were on display at a museum 100 years from now. What would people see? What objects from your life would help future generations understand American life as you know it?

_____

_____

_____

HISTORY NOTEBOOK | **UNIT 7** | FULBRIGHT-NATIONAL GEOGRAPHIC EXPLORER
Ari Beser

Stories don't just entertain us, they also educate us, help preserve our cultures, and teach us about history. Fulbright-National Geographic Explorer Ari Beser uses the power of storytelling to bring to light the experiences of the atomic bomb survivors of World War II.

1. Reading Check What events led to Ari Beser's decision to investigate the stories of the bomb survivors?

_____

_____

2. One of the interviewees says to Beser, "How do you always get me to say things I've never said before?" What personal qualities and skills do you think a person who does what Beser is doing would need to have? Why are those qualities important?

_____

_____

_____

3. **Ask Questions** If you were to interview one of the atomic bomb survivors, what questions would you want to ask? How would you get the person to share his or her personal story?

_____

_____

_____

4. **Analyze Language Use** What do you think Beser means when he says, "We are each other's history"?

_____

_____

_____

5. Beser also says, "This just happens to be my family's story." What is your family's story? Tell your story below.

_____

_____

_____

_____

6. Imagine Ari Beser is doing a talk at your school and you are assigned to introduce him before his talk. How would you introduce him?

_____

_____

Go online to view photographs of the Tuskegee Airmen and learn about their contribution to the war. Then review the questions below and record your thoughts.

1. **Evaluate** After viewing the photos and reading the captions, what were you most surprised to learn about the Tuskegee Airmen? What was surprising about it?

_____

_____

_____

2. The Tuskegee Airmen broke racial barriers to become pilots. What personal qualities do you think a person in pilot training for the Tuskegee Airmen would need to have? List three qualities and explain why they would be important.

_____

_____

_____

_____

4. Go online for more information about the Tuskegee Airmen. What other photographs would you add to this gallery? Explain why you think the photos you chose should be added.

_____

_____

_____

_____

_____

5. **Make Inferences** The Tuskegee Airmen were honored in 2006 with a Congressional Gold Medal. Why do you think it took so many years after their service for them to receive this award?

_____

_____

_____

_____

6. **Ask Questions** After reviewing all the photographs in this gallery, what more do you want to know about the Tuskegee Airmen? List your questions below.

_____

_____

_____

HISTORY NOTEBOOK | **UNIT 7** | AMERICAN STORY ONLINE
Cold War Spy Technology

NATIONAL GEOGRAPHIC
L E A R N I N G

Spy technology has a long history, starting with the Revolutionary War—but it's come a long way since then. Learn about how it was used during the Cold War in this American Story.

1. **Reading Check** What were some of the capabilities of the U-2 spy plane? Why would a plane with those features be needed?

_____

_____

_____

2. **Evaluate** Of the spy technologies used during the Cold War, which one do you think was most crucial or most effective for the U.S. government's purposes? Explain why.

_____

_____

_____

3. **Form and Support Opinions** Would you have wanted to be a spy during the Cold War? If so, what appeals to you about it and what gadgets would you have wanted to use? If not, why not?

_____

_____

_____

4. What fact were you most surprised to learn about in this American Story? What was surprising about it?

_____

_____

_____

5. **Make Generalizations** In what ways did the Cold War help shape spy technology?

_____

_____

_____

6. What spy technology would you create today? Find out about a current event in the news and create your own type of spy technology that could be used to gather more information.

_____

_____

_____

HISTORY NOTEBOOK | UNIT **7** | **AMERICAN GALLERY**
The Korean War

Explore this collection of poignant photographs detailing the Korean War.
Then capture what you learned using the prompts below.

1. **Describe** If you had to pick three adjectives to describe the Korean War based on the photographs in this American Gallery, what would those three adjectives be?

_____

_____

2. **Evaluate** Which photograph in this collection do you find most interesting or compelling and why?

_____

_____

3. **Make Inferences** Select one of the photos with soldiers in it and study the men. Write a few sentences describing their facial expressions, gestures, body language, and surroundings. What do these nonverbal signals tell you that the caption doesn't? What do they reveal about the tone or mood?

_____

_____

_____

4. **Ask Questions** Pick the photo that raised the most questions for you, and record a few of the questions you have about it below.

_____

_____

_____

5. Review the photo of Eisenhower visiting the front lines. What does the photo convey about the type of leader Eisenhower was? Do you see him as a role model? Why or why not?

_____

_____

_____

6. Pick one of the photographs shown in this American Gallery, and prepare a 2-minute presentation about it to share with the class. Use the caption in the gallery to begin with, and then go online for more information. Include additional photos related to the one you chose in your presentation.

_____

_____

_____

_____

HISTORY NOTEBOOK | **UNIT 7** | **AMERICAN STORY**
The Birth of Rock and Roll

NATIONAL GEOGRAPHIC
L E A R N I N G

The birth of rock and roll wasn't just about the music—it was about the identity of a generation. Read about how rock and roll music started in this American Story and then record your responses to the questions below.

1. **Reading Check** How did rock and roll music get its start, and from what genre of music did it emerge?

_____

_____

2. **Explore Identity** Rock and roll music reflected the emergence of teen culture. What type of music do you think represents the teenage identity today, and how so?

_____

_____

_____

3. **Ask Questions** You read about several legends of rock and roll in this American Story. Who do you want to learn more about and why? Write three questions you might have for your selected rock legend.

_____

_____

_____

4. Review the excerpt from *Billboard's* Top 50 Best Sellers in Stores list (shown in the Top of the List feature). Pick one song from the list and listen to a recording of it. You should be able to access an excerpt online. Then write a music review of the song from the perspective of a music journalist.

_____

_____

_____

_____

5. The Rock and Roll Hall of Fame honors musicians who "founded, changed, and revolutionized rock and roll." Since 1986, hundreds of musicians have been inducted into the hall of fame. Who would you choose to be in the Rock and Roll Hall of Fame? Explain your selection.

_____

_____

_____

HISTORY NOTEBOOK | UNIT **7** | **REID ON THE ROAD**
The Motown Sound

Visit the legendary home of Motown with National Geographic Digital Nomad Robert Reid. After watching the video, use the prompts below to record your thoughts.

1. **Identify Main Ideas and Details** How did Motown get its name, and who created the name?

_____

_____

_____

2. **Identify** What defines the classic Motown sound, and why is it so popular?

_____

_____

_____

3. **Explore Identity** How did Motown influence American culture and society in the 1960s? What does the music of Motown say about American identity at that time?

_____

_____

_____

4. What part of the Motown story did you find most interesting? Explain. What do you want to find out more about?

_____

_____

_____

5. If you were to create a music business like Motown, what would you call it and why? What type of music would your music label feature?

_____

_____

_____

6. **Evaluate** Listen to music by one of the artists mentioned in the video. Write a review of the song you listened to, describing the sound and style. Note what you like about the song and what you don't like.

_____

_____

_____

_____

HISTORY NOTEBOOK **UNIT 7** **THROUGH THE LENS**
Cars & American Culture

NATIONAL GEOGRAPHIC
L E A R N I N G

Review the photographs in this Through the Lens look at cars and the American culture. Then write your responses to the prompts below.

1. **Reading Check** Over the years, what has owning a car represented?

_____

_____

2. **Evaluate** Pick one of the photographs shown in this lesson and use your own words to explain what that photo reveals about the American culture in the time period shown. Why did you pick the photo you chose?

_____

_____

_____

3. **Make Inferences** Why are cars considered a significant part of American culture? How do they define American identity?

_____

_____

_____

4. Select one of the photographs, and prepare a two-minute presentation to share with the class about the story behind the car shown. Use the caption to begin with, then go online for more information if needed. Record your notes below.

_____

_____

_____

_____

5. **Design Your Own** The photographs show a variety of cars from different time periods in the United States. What do you think cars will look like in 10, 20, or even 50 years? Use the space below to design your own car of the future. Be sure to include descriptions and functions of different parts of the car.

_____

_____

_____

_____

_____

HISTORY NOTEBOOK | **UNIT 7** | CURATING HISTORY **National Baseball Hall of Fame and Museum, Cooperstown, New York**

Explore the objects from the National Baseball Hall of Fame and Museum, and then answer the questions below.

1. **Reading Check** What type of artifacts are featured at this museum?

_____

_____

2. **Make Inferences** Pick one of the artifacts shown in this lesson and use your own words to explain what that artifact reveals about baseball. Why did you pick the artifact you chose?

_____

_____

3. Think of your favorite sport or hobby. What collection of artifacts would you put together to celebrate your sport or hobby? Explain why you chose the objects you put together.

_____

_____

4. Some museums and some artifacts don't appeal to everyone, and that's to be expected. Would you want to visit this museum to see these objects? If so, why? If not, why not?

_____

_____

5. A bronze plaque such as the one shown here for Hank Aaron is made for every inductee into the Baseball Hall of Fame. Who do you think should be inducted into the hall of fame and why?

_____

_____

6. **Describe** Jeff Idelson says, "There's nothing better than sitting at a baseball game." Have you ever been to a baseball game? If so, what was that experience like and do you agree with Idelson's statement? If not, what other types of sporting events have you been to or would want to go to?

_____

_____

_____

7. Think about what you already know about baseball. What objects from baseball today would you add to the museum? If you aren't sure, do a little online research to find out more about key players and events in baseball today.

_____

_____

HISTORY NOTEBOOK UNIT **7** AMERICAN GALLERY
Consumer America

The 1950s led to a boom in American consumerism as shown in this American Gallery. After viewing the photographs, use the prompts below to think about how consumerism grew and what it looks like today.

1. **Identify** What do these visuals as a group convey about the American identity during the 1950s?

_____

_____

2. Read the caption for the photo of the women shopping at the supermarket. As noted, cars and suburbs changed how and where people shopped for groceries. Today there are even more ways to shop. What other technologies and cultural shifts have changed the way people shop today, and how do people shop now?

_____

_____

3. Which photograph from this gallery did you find most interesting and why?

_____

_____

4. Review the photo of the electronics kit. Science and space influenced many of the toys created in the 1950s. What are some popular toys today? What topics, current events, and pop culture of today influenced these popular toys? Put together a photo gallery of the trendy toys of the last ten years and explain why you think they are popular.

_____

_____

_____

5. **Compare and Contrast** Select one photo from the gallery to compare with its modern-day equivalent. Find a photo of the same type of object or situation in today's culture. Then compare the two photos. Which photo did you choose from the gallery, and what is today's version of that object, action, or product? How are they similar and how are they different?

_____

_____

_____

6. **Form and Support Opinions** How do you think American consumerism has changed since the 1950s? Explain why and support your answer with examples.

_____

_____

_____

UNIT WRAP-UP
A New World Power

This unit, A New World Power, focuses on the emergence of the United States as a new world power, from the time of the New Deal to the buildup of the next world war to World War II. Use the questions below to think about what you learned in Unit 7.

A. After Reading Once you've completed Unit 7, revisit the chapters to select the topic that you find most interesting.

1. What is the topic I found most interesting in this unit?

_____

2. How or why does this topic interest me?

_____

3. What are some of the most important take-aways I got from this unit?

_____

_____

4. How does this topic relate to my life, my family, my community, and my identity?

_____

_____

_____

B. American's Shocking Propaganda Machine Review the article and respond to the questions below.

3. What is the subject of the article?

_____

4. What was the purpose of the U.S. political propaganda during the war?

_____

_____

5. How does this article connect with the focus of the unit? Why do you think the editors of this U.S. History program selected this article for this unit?

_____

_____

_____

C. Unit Activities As you prepare for your unit inquiry and the learning framework, record any thoughts, ideas, or lingering questions below.

_____

_____

_____

HISTORY NOTEBOOK | UNIT **8** | AMERICAN STORY
Civil Rights Stories

NATIONAL GEOGRAPHIC
L E A R N I N G

Learn about the civil rights movement and some of the key events and players in the fight for civil rights. Then respond to the prompts below.

---

1. Reading Check Why was there a Civil Rights movement?

_____

_____

---

2. What do you think was the most significant achievement of the Civil Rights movement? Explain your selection.

_____

_____

_____

3. Turn and Talk Do you think protest marches are an effective way to create change? Why or why not? Which strategy employed by civil rights activists do you think was most effective? Discuss with a partner and record your notes below.

_____

_____

_____

4. Identify You learned about different stories of inequality and discrimination. What inequalities continue to exist? What groups do you think still have not achieved protection under the law? What changes do you think can be made to provide a more just and equal society?

_____

_____

_____

5. Describe a time you felt discriminated against or a time you discriminated against someone.

_____

_____

_____

6. Evaluate In what ways have civil rights improved since the Civil Rights Movement? Have civil rights and issues such as racism, women's rights, and religious discrimination gotten better or worse over the years? Explain your answer.

_____

_____

_____

AMERICAN VOICES
Thurgood Marshall

Thurgood Marshall was a civil rights lawyer and the first African-American justice to serve on the U.S. Supreme Court. Review the American Voices lesson and then record your responses to the questions below.

1. **Reading Check** What role did Thurgood Marshall play in the Civil Rights movement?

_____

_____

2. Read the quotation by Thurgood Marshall. What does he mean by saying that to protest is in the foundation of our democracy? Do you agree or disagree with his statement? Explain your reasoning.

_____

_____

_____

3. **Identify** Marshall won 29 of the 32 cases he argued before the Supreme Court. What skills contributed to his success as a civil rights lawyer? What personal qualities do you think someone who does what Marshall does would need to have?

_____

_____

_____

4. Do you see Marshall as a role model? Is he someone you would try to emulate? If so, why? If not, why not?

_____

_____

_____

5. **Form and Support Opinions** Thurgood Marshall was truly a remarkable leader in the advancements of civil rights. Support that statement with your own opinions about his accomplishments—or explain why you aren't all that impressed with him.

_____

_____

_____

6. **Make Predictions** How do you think Marshall would react to the Supreme Court today? What advice do you think he would give you and your classmates if he were still alive?

_____

_____

HISTORY NOTEBOOK | **UNIT 8** | AMERICAN GALLERY
The Freedom Riders

Go online to learn about and view photographs of the Freedom Riders, civil rights activists who rode interstate buses through the south to protest segregation.

1. **Identify** If you had to choose one photograph in this gallery that most powerfully tells the story of the Freedom Riders, which one would you choose and why?

_____

_____

2. Given what you learned about the civil rights movement, would you have gone on one of the Freedom Rides? Why or why not? Do you think this strategy was effective?

_____

_____

_____

3. **Draw Conclusions** Why were the Freedom Riders successful?

_____

_____

_____

4. Create your own gallery to tell the story of the Freedom Riders. Start by picking one photograph and caption from this gallery, and then add at least four more photos you found about the Freedom Riders. Write captions for your photos.

_____

_____

_____

_____

_____

5. **Debate the Issue** Pair up with a classmate and discuss the following statement: *The federal government should have stepped in sooner and offered full protection for the Freedom Riders.* To prepare for your debate, take notes below, provide sound arguments, and use evidence to support your opinion.

_____

_____

_____

_____

_____

After years of challenges and war in the United States, the 1960s ushered in a counterculture movement—one of peace, love, and freedom. Read about the counterculture and its lasting impression on American society, and then record your thoughts using the prompts below.

1. **Reading Check** What was the counterculture movement of the 1960s?

_____

_____

2. **Make Connections** How did hippies influence trends in 1960s culture and politics? In what ways do you think the counterculture movement influenced trends that exist today?

_____

_____

3. **Analyze Cause and Effect** The Summer of Love was seen as "emblematic of the counterculture." What were some positive and some negative effects of the time period?

_____

_____

4. Review Timothy Leary's quotation. What is he referring to by the "turned-on underground"? And what does he mean by people "dropping out"?

_____

_____

_____

5. **Connect to Today** Music is an important part of any culture, and its significance to the counterculture was no exception. Think about popular music today and the music you like to listen to.

What type of music, which songs, and which artists do you think are the voice of your generation? And what do those songs and artists convey about American culture today?

_____

_____

_____

Imagine you were putting together a music festival. What would be the theme of the festival that you think represents a movement in the Untied States today? What would you name the festival, and which artists would you invite to perform?

_____

_____

_____

AMERICAN VOICES
John Fitzgerald Kennedy

NATIONAL GEOGRAPHIC
L E A R N I N G

Learn about the life—and death—of the 35th president of the United States, John F. Kennedy. Then record your thoughts on the questions below.

1. **Reading Check** Why did Joe Kennedy, Sr., feel he could not achieve a higher role in politics, and what did he do to remedy that?

_____

_____

2. **Evaluate** What was the single fact or idea about John F. Kennedy that most surprised you, and how so?

_____

_____

_____

3. Do you see Kennedy as a role model? Is he someone you would try to emulate? If so, why? If not, why?

_____

_____

_____

4. What question would you most like to ask Kennedy if you were face to face right now? And how do you imagine he would answer it?

_____

_____

_____

5. **Make Inferences** Why do you think Jackie Kennedy modeled JFK's funeral after Abraham Lincoln's funeral?

_____

_____

_____

6. **Form and Support Opinions** Kennedy says, "A man may die, nations may rise and fall, but an idea lives on." Do you agree with that statement? Why or why not? Can you think of an example to support that statement?

_____

_____

_____

_____

HISTORY NOTEBOOK | UNIT 8

NATIONAL GEOGRAPHIC EXPLORER
Leslie Dewan

Nuclear engineer and environmentalist Leslie Dewan has a new plan for harnessing the power of nuclear energy. Learn about her work and answer the questions below.

---

1. Reading Check Why was nuclear power first developed?

_____

_____

---

2. Describe What caused the nuclear disasters such as Three Mile Island? How did those disasters influence energy development and future use of nuclear power?

_____

_____

_____

3. How does National Geographic Explorer Leslie Dewan think she can "save the world with nuclear power"?

_____

_____

4. What personal qualities do you think a person who does what Dewan does would need to have? List three qualities and explain why they would be important.

_____

_____

_____

5. Ask Questions What more do you want to know about Dewan and the work she is doing? Write three questions below that you would want to ask her.

_____

_____

_____

6. Discuss and Debate Form a group with three other classmates and discuss the advantages and disadvantages of nuclear energy. Then stage a quick debate on Dewan's ending quote about the need for nuclear power. Have two of you argue the side for and the other two argue the side against the statement. Record notes for each argument below.

_____

_____

_____

_____

HISTORY NOTEBOOK | **UNIT 8** **THROUGH THE LENS**
David Guttenfelder

Read about National Geographic photographer David Guttenfelder and his historic trip to Cuba in this Through the Lens feature. Explore your understanding using the prompts below.

1. **Reading Check** For what purpose did National Geographic photographer David Guttenfelder go to Cuba?

_____

_____

2. **Interpret Maps** Use a map in your textbook or classroom map to locate Cuba. Figure out roughly how far this place is from where you live. Would you want to visit Cuba? Write a few sentences below about why you might or might not want to visit.

_____

_____

3. **Evaluate** How does the photo help you understand what it's like to live in Cuba? What does it tell you about the Cuban experience?

_____

_____

_____

4. Conduct some online research to find other photos taken by Guttenfelder. Which photos did you find most interesting and why? What do his photos reveal about his subjects?

_____

_____

_____

5. **Ask Questions** This Through the Lens lesson reveals a small part of Cuba and its history and culture. What more do you want to find out about Cuba? List three questions below.

_____

_____

_____

6. One photo can say a lot. In this lesson, the photo tells a story of Cuba. Find one photo that you think tells a story about life in the United States. Describe the photo and the story it tells about the American experience. Be prepared to share your photo and story with the class.

_____

_____

_____

HISTORY NOTEBOOK | UNIT 8 | CURATING HISTORY National Civil Rights Museum, Memphis, Tennessee

NATIONAL GEOGRAPHIC L E A R N I N G

Museums are meant to educate, inform, and inspire. The National Civil Rights Museum's collection of objects tells the story of African-American history. Explore the lesson and then answer the questions below.

1. Reading Check What types of exhibits does the National Civil Rights Museum focus on?

_____

_____

2. Make Inferences Why do you think the grounds of the Lorraine Motel were chosen as the site of the museum?

_____

_____

3. This collection of artifacts is focused on African-American history from the time period of the civil rights movement. Do a little research online to come up with photos of some additional artifacts from the Civil Rights movement. Find a way to share the artifacts you found with your classmates, and be prepared to talk for 30 seconds about each one. Record your notes on the objects below.

_____

_____

4. Form and Support Opinions Which artifact shown do you find most interesting, and what do you find most interesting about it?

_____

_____

5. You can learn a lot about a time period or a culture or society by examining what humans have left behind. Imagine it's 100 years from now, and identify an object from your life today that you think would help future generations understand American life as you know it. List the object you chose below. Explain what you think it reveals about American life today.

_____

_____

6. Connect to Today Which objects from today would you add to this collection? Explain why you chose the objects you did.

_____

_____

_____

HISTORY NOTEBOOK | **UNIT 8** | **AMERICAN GALLERY**
The Space Race

NATIONAL GEOGRAPHIC
L E A R N I N G

Go online to view this American Gallery's collection of photographs about the great space race between the United States and the Soviet Union.

1. **Identify** After reviewing the photographs and captions, what were you most surprised to learn about the space race?

_____

_____

2. **Explore Identity** The space race captured the attention of the American public. Study the photograph of the crowd at New York's Grand Central Station and describe what the atmosphere must have been like during the time of the six Project Mercury spaceflights. How would you describe the American identity during the space race?

_____

_____

_____

3. All seven of the Mercury astronauts were former test pilots. What skills and qualities do you think were needed to become an astronaut at that time? Are the same skills are needed for astronauts today? What other skills might be needed?

_____

_____

_____

4. **Draw Conclusions** What conclusions can you draw about the role of women in space research and exploration during the space race?

_____

_____

_____

5. Based on what you have learned, would you have wanted to be an astronaut during the space race? Why or why not? Would you want to be one now?

_____

_____

_____

6. **Ask Questions** What more do you want to learn about the space missions, NASA, or any of the key people featured in this gallery? List your questions below.

_____

_____

Go online to read this American Story about the Vietnam Wall—a memorial to all those who served in the Vietnam War. Then answer the questions below.

1. **Reading Check** What was the goal of the Vietnam memorial and why would the VVMF have added fourth design criteria?

   _____

   _____

   _____

2. **Describe** Have you ever visited the Vietnam Wall or another memorial like it? If so, what was that experience like? If not, which memorial would you want to see and why?

   _____

   _____

   _____

3. **Explore Identity** What do you think the Vietnam Wall—and other memorials in the United States—adds to an understanding of our American identity?

   _____

   _____

   _____

4. **Form and Support Opinions** Not everyone was a fan of the winning Vietnam memorial design. Go online to find out more about Maya Lin's design and the controversy surrounding it. What do you think of her design? Do you think she should have won? If so, why? If not, what type of memorial should've been made?

   _____

   _____

   _____

5. Imagine you were asked to design a Vietnam War memorial in your community. Based on what you have learned about the Vietnam War, what type of memorial would you create? Write your vision and goals for the memorial below, and include a description of your design.

   _____

   _____

   _____

   _____

HISTORY NOTEBOOK | **UNIT 8** | *REID ON THE ROAD*
Haight-Ashbury

Join National Geographic Digital Nomad Robert Reid as he explores the Haight-Ashbury neighborhood in San Francisco, California to learn about the hippie culture.

1. Identify What is a hippie and what ideals do they represent?

_____

_____

_____

2. Connect to Geography Why are hippies commonly associated with the Haight-Ashbury neighborhood in California? How did geography play a role in the hippie movement?

_____

_____

_____

3. How does this video help you understand the counterculture of the 1960s?

_____

_____

_____

4. Connect to Today Some ideals of the hippie lifestyle as well as the clothing styles have become ingrained in today's popular culture. In what ways do you think the hippie culture is still reflected today? What other past countercultures have had lasting effects on American popular culture?

_____

_____

_____

_____

5. Explore Identity In the video, Reid discusses symbols that have been associated with the hippie identity. He also discusses other ways hippies express themselves, such as through clothing and colors. What symbols would you use as a visual representation of your identity? Take a moment to journal on the ideals and values that are important to you and then identify the symbols that would best express those values and your identity.

_____

_____

_____

_____

HISTORY NOTEBOOK **UNIT 8**

AMERICAN GALLERY
Reporters Go to War

Soldiers weren't the only ones serving the military. During the Vietnam War, journalists joined the troops to capture the action and convey the realities of war home to the American people. Review the photographs and then record your thoughts below.

1. **Evaluate** How do these photographs help you understand the role of journalists during wartime?

_____

_____

2. **Form and Support Opinions** Study the photo of journalist Peter Arnett. Do you agree with him that "the story must come before safety"? Why or why not?

_____

_____

3. Journalists faced many challenges reporting on the Vietnam War. Despite the risks, Ron Nessen noted that the war shaped who he became as a person. After studying the photos and captions, what aspects of being a wartime journalist appeal to you? What aspects might not be appealing for you?

_____

_____

4. **Turn and Talk** Discuss with a partner the photojournalist's dilemma: when to document a tragedy and when to step in and help. What would you do? Record your notes below.

_____

_____

_____

5. **Make Inferences** You learned about several reporters who were arrested or injured in the line of duty yet returned over and over again to the battlefields. Why would they want to go back to such dangerous situations?

_____

_____

_____

6. **Discuss and Debate** Form a group with three other classmates and discuss whether or not journalists should be allowed to join troops on missions. Then stage a quick debate on the statements listed below. Have two of you argue one statement and the other two argue the opposing statement. To prepare for your debate, explain why you agree with the statement you chose and provide sound arguments for your side.

   • *Reporters should not be in embedded with military troops during wartime.*
   • *It's important for reporters to join military troops when reporting on wars.*

_____

_____

HISTORY NOTEBOOK UNIT **8**

AMERICAN STORY
One Giant Leap

NATIONAL GEOGRAPHIC
L E A R N I N G

July 20, 1969, is a day that will forever live in history—on this day, Neil Armstrong became the first man to land on the moon as part of the Apollo 11 mission. Explore this historic event and the U.S. space program, and then record your thoughts below.

1. **Reading Check** Why were Americans concerned that the Soviets were more advanced in space technology?

_____

_____

_____

2. **Evaluate** What did you find most surprising or interesting in this American Story and why?

_____

_____

3. **Make Inferences** NASA hired women, African Americans, and immigrants at a time when most companies still discriminated against women and minorities. Why do you think NASA hired women, African Americans, and immigrants for positions that were usually reserved for white men during the 1950s and 60s?

_____

_____

4. **Explore Identity** Based on President John F. Kennedy's speech, how did he describe the American identity during the age of space exploration? How would you describe the American identity now? Why has it changed or stayed the same?

_____

_____

5. **Debate Spending** Which of the statements below do you agree with? Pair up with a classmate who chose the opposing statement and stage a quick debate. To prepare for your debate, take notes below, explain why you agree with the statement you chose, and provide sound arguments for the advantages or disadvantages of further space exploration.

We should increase government spending on space exploration for Mars research.

We should decrease government spending on space exploration for Mars research.

_____

_____

6. If the United States were to send people to Mars, explore Europa, or go to the moon again, what existing technologies would be needed and what new technologies would need to be developed?

_____

_____

HISTORY NOTEBOOK | UNIT **8** | **THROUGH THE LENS**
Angélica Dass

NATIONAL GEOGRAPHIC
L E A R N I N G

When you think of your skin color, what color would you say it is? There are so many different tones and variations of skin color, it's not a matter of black, brown, or white. Look through the lens of Brazilian artist Angélica Dass's Humanæ project to see people's actual skin tones represented by Pantone colors.

1. Reading Check What does Angélica Dass hope to accomplish with her Humanæ project?

_____

_____

2. Describe How would you describe the expressions on the people's faces in the photos? Why would they show that specific expression?

_____

_____

_____

_____

3. Would you want to be a part of this project? Why or why not? And in what way?

_____

_____

_____

_____

4. Ask Questions This Through the Lens lesson reveals a small part of the Humanæ project and Dass's work. What more do you want to find out about the project? About Dass's work? List your questions below.

_____

_____

_____

_____

5. Explore Identity Often we've touched on American identity. This project focuses on the human identity. What do you think Dass's photography conveys about the human identity?

_____

_____

_____

_____

HISTORY NOTEBOOK | **UNIT 8**

THROUGH THE LENS, AMERICAN PLACES
Stonewall National Monument

NATIONAL GEOGRAPHIC
L E A R N I N G

Learn how the Stonewall Inn in New York City became a national monument, and then respond to the questions below.

1. Reading Check What is the Stonewall National Monument and why is it significant?

_____

_____

_____

2. Summarize How did rights for the lesbian, gay, bisexual, transgender, and queer (LGBTQ) community evolve from the mid-20th century to the mid-1970s?

_____

_____

_____

_____

3. Compare and Contrast How are LGBTQ rights different today than they were in 1969? Conduct online research, if necessary. Are rights better or worse today, and how so?

_____

_____

_____

_____

4. Form and Support Opinions President Barack Obama made the Stonewall Inn a national monument in 2016. Do you agree that the site should be a national monument? Why or why not?

_____

_____

_____

_____

5. What's going on in the world today? Go online to read more about current events in the news. Identify a major event that has taken place in the last 10 years that you think should be memorialized in some way. Which place related to the event should be made into a national monument or historic site? Explain why.

_____

_____

_____

Name _____

Study the photographs and captions in this American Gallery to learn about key moments and significant leaders in the women's movement. Then respond to the questions below.

1. **Identify** What do the photographs and visuals tell you about the women's movement in the past and today? What other objects from today would you add to this gallery?

_____

_____

2. **Compare and Contrast** Study the photos and captions of Gloria Steinem and Phyllis Schafly. Both were leaders in the women's movement. How are they similar and how are they different?

_____

_____

3. **Make Inferences** Why do you think Phyllis Schafly was successful in stopping the ERA?

_____

_____

4. **Turn and Talk** By 1977, 35 states ratified the ERA but 3 more states needed to approve it in order for it to be added to the Constitution. Fifteen states did not ratify the ERA before the 1982 deadline. Discuss with a partner reasons for approving the ERA and reasons against it. How would you persuade state legislators to vote one way or the other?

_____

_____

_____

5. You learned about several key leaders and events in the women's movement. Select one of the women or events featured in this gallery, and do some online research to find out more about the leader or event. Create a short presentation that tells the story about your selected person or event to share with your class. Write a short paragraph describing the person or event, and add additional visuals to your presentation.

_____

_____

_____

6. **Form and Support Opinions** Do you think women have made progress in their fight for rights? How so? If not, what do you think needs to change? Also, who do you think has been most effective in advancing women's rights and why?

_____

_____

_____

UNIT WRAP-UP
Years of Turbulence

This unit, Years of Turbulence, describes a tumultuous time in U.S. history. From assassinations of national leaders to protest movements to a difficult war, the United States experienced violence and chaos that divided the nation. Use the questions below to think about what you learned in Unit 8.

A. After Reading Once you've completed Unit 8, revisit the chapters to select the topic that you find most interesting.

1. What is the topic I found most interesting in this unit?

_____

2. How or why does this topic interest me?

_____

3. What are some of the most important take-aways you got from this unit?

_____

_____

4. How does this topic relate to my life, my family, my community, and my identity?

_____

_____

B. Who Was Jim Crow? Review the article and respond to the questions below.

5. What is the subject of the article?

_____

6. Where did the name Jim Crow originate from and what did it come to mean?

_____

_____

7. How does this article connect with the focus of the unit? Why do you think the editors of this U.S. History program selected this article for this unit?

_____

_____

_____

C. Unit Activities As you prepare for your unit inquiry and the learning framework, record any thoughts, ideas, or lingering questions below.

_____

_____

_____

HISTORY NOTEBOOK | UNIT **9** | AMERICAN STORY ONLINE
The Iranian Hostage Crisis

Go online to read this American Story about the Iranian hostage crisis and respond to the questions below.

1. Reading Check How did the U.S. government try to persuade the Iranian government to release the hostages?

_____

_____

_____

2. What do you already know about the Iranian hostage crisis? What more do you want to learn about it?

_____

_____

_____

3. Analyze Cause and Effect What effect did the hostage crisis have on the news media and the American public?

_____

_____

_____

_____

4. Imagine you are one of the hostages. Write a journal entry about what one day in captivity might be like. What strategies would you use to cope with the worry, frustration, and boredom?

_____

_____

_____

5. Make Inferences Why was the timing of the release considered an "intentional slap" against Jimmy Carter?

_____

_____

_____

6. Form and Support Opinions Do you think the strategies employed by the U.S. government to release the hostages were effective? If so, why? If not, what might have been more effective?

_____

_____

_____

THROUGH THE LENS
Paul Nicklen

You've learned about the growth of the environmental movement, environmental policies, conservation groups, and controversies. Now study the photograph and text in this Through the Lens feature. Record your thoughts below.

1. **Reading Check** What does National Geographic photographer Paul Nicklen hope to achieve through his photographs?

_____

_____

2. **Describe** Review the photograph of Denali National Park. How would you describe it to someone who hasn't seen the park or this photo? What does this photo reveal about the American landscape?

_____

_____

_____

3. **Evaluate** Review the photograph in terms of photographic technique. For example, is it a close-up or taken from a distance? Is there a certain angle that the photographer took that makes the photo special? What makes this particular photograph compelling or surprising?

_____

_____

_____

_____

4. **Debate the Issue** Pair up with a classmate. Imagine one of you is an environmental protection advocate, and the other is a property rights activist. Decide which person will take each side, and then stage a short debate. To prepare for your debate, take notes below and include evidence to support your opinion.

_____

_____

_____

5. Imagine National Geographic photographer Paul Nicklen is doing a talk at your school and you are assigned to introduce him before his talk. How would you introduce him?

_____

_____

_____

From planting trees to protest marches, people have tried various ways to raise environmental awareness and save the earth. Review the images in this American Gallery to learn about how people have protected the environment. Then record your thoughts on the questions below.

1. Make Generalizations What story about the United States do these images as a group tell?

_____

_____

_____

2. Which photograph do you find most interesting, and what do you find most interesting about it?

_____

_____

_____

3. Describe For each photograph, write down 3 adjectives that you think describe the mood, purpose, or central idea of that photo.

_____

_____

_____

_____

_____

4. Compare and Contrast Review the two photographs of the Cuyahoga River and notice the differences and similarities between the river in 1969 and the river in 2011. Conduct online research to find before and after photographs of another river or a lake in the United States that was either polluted and is now cleaned up or vice versa. Compare and contrast the photographs and write your notes below.

_____

_____

_____

_____

5. What do you learn from these photographs that you wouldn't learn from a written description of conservation efforts?

_____

_____

_____

_____

HISTORY NOTEBOOK | UNIT 9

AMERICAN STORY ONLINE
The Gulf Wars

NATIONAL GEOGRAPHIC
L E A R N I N G

Go online to learn about the first and second Gulf Wars. After reading this American Story, record your thoughts below.

1. Reading Check What events led to the start of the second Gulf War?

_____

_____

_____

2. Make Inferences Why would the United States get involved in the Gulf Wars? Of what interest would it be to the United States?

_____

_____

_____

_____

3. The Gulf Wars brought about new technological developments. What effects did those advancements have on the war? What do you think is the greatest technological advancement made during the Gulf Wars and why?

_____

_____

_____

_____

4. Synthesize Explain the evolution of warfare from World War I to the Gulf Wars. How did warfare change over time and what remained the same?

_____

_____

_____

_____

5. Connect to Today You've read about the United States' relationship with Iraq during the Gulf Wars. What is the relationship between the two countries like today? Do a little online research to find out how relations between the United States and Iraq are today. Record your notes here.

_____

_____

_____

_____

HISTORY NOTEBOOK | UNIT **9** | *REID ON THE ROAD*
Internet Research

How did people conduct research before the Internet? National Geographic Digital Nomad Robert Reid finds out when he visits the Computer History Museum. After viewing the video, answer the questions below.

1. Summarize What led to the development of the worldwide web?

_____

_____

2. As you watch the video, write down three ideas that you want to remember from the video, and explain why you think they are important.

_____

_____

3. Evaluate What did you find most interesting or surprising about this video? Explain why below.

_____

_____

_____

4. Make Inferences Computer History Museum Internet Curator Mark Webber describes the past method for conducting research, which was the same method for many years. Why do you think the past research method lasted so long? Why did it change?

_____

_____

_____

5. Make a list of all the ways or reasons people use the Internet today. Don't think too much about your answers, just list the first ones that come to mind. Review your list and then write how people conducted those tasks before the Internet.

_____

_____

_____

6. Turn and Talk Discuss with a partner the role of the Internet and its benefits and drawbacks. What do you think is the biggest advantage of the Internet? What do you think is the biggest disadvantage of it? Record your notes below.

_____

_____

_____

HISTORY NOTEBOOK | **UNIT 9**

CURATING HISTORY
The Newseum, Washington, D.C.

NATIONAL GEOGRAPHIC
L E A R N I N G

Study the photographs of artifacts and exhibits at the Newseum in Washington, D.C., and then answer the questions below.

1. **Reading Check** What type of museum is Newseum, and what is its main focus?

_____

_____

2. **Visual Literacy** To develop your skills of observation, pick one of the objects or photographs in the gallery and write 3 questions you think you should be asking as you look at the item. If you know the answers to your questions, write the answers too.

_____

_____

_____

3. **Describe** Based on the artifacts and exhibits you see in this lesson, what other historic event covered in the news would you expect to find featured in this museum? What objects would you expect to find for that news event?

_____

_____

_____

_____

4. Some museums and some artifacts don't appeal to everyone, and that's to be expected. Would you want to visit this museum to see these objects? If so, why? If not, why not?

_____

_____

_____

_____

5. Pick one of the freedoms mentioned in this lesson. Then create your own exhibit that represents that freedom. Which freedom did you pick and why? What news event and objects are included in your collection? Would you make the exhibit interactive and if so, how?

_____

_____

_____

_____

Name _____

Explore the history of the Berlin Wall through this collection of photographs, and then record your responses to the questions below.

1. **Describe** As you review all the photographs in this American Gallery, what are your first impressions of what life was like when the Berlin Wall was built? What adjectives would you use to describe the Berlin Wall?

_____

_____

_____

2. What do you learn from these photographs that you wouldn't learn from a written description of the Berlin Wall?

_____

_____

_____

_____

3. **Draw Conclusions** Review the photograph of the wall of East German soldiers. Based on the expressions on people's faces, what can you tell about the mood of the crowd behind them? How do you think the East German soldiers are feeling and what details indicate their mood?

_____

_____

_____

_____

4. **Ask Questions** Which photograph in the gallery do you want to learn more about? Pick one and write at least three questions you have about that photograph.

_____

_____

_____

_____

5. This gallery of photographs tells the story of the division between East and West Germany by the Berlin Wall. What photographs would you put together to tell the story of the unification of East and West Germany? Conduct online research to find images that show life during and after the unification. Create a slideshow presentation using at least 5 to 6 images, include captions, and be prepared to present it to the class.

_____

_____

_____

_____

HISTORY NOTEBOOK | UNIT **9** | AMERICAN STORY
The First Environmentalists

After reading this American Story about Native Americans' relationship with the environment, answer the questions below.

1. Reading Check How did pre-contact Native Americans shape the natural ecosystem?

_____

_____

_____

2. What common themes do you notice in this American Story?

_____

_____

_____

3. Analyze Language Use Review historian Louis S. Warren's quotation. What did he mean by the phrase that they were "a people without history"? Why would they be without a history?

_____

_____

_____

4. Form and Support Opinions As the feature notes, sometimes tribes' cultural practices conflict with conservation groups. The Makah Indians have a time-honored tradition of whaling, yet environmentalists say some whale populations are in danger. How important is it to keep cultural practices alive?

_____

_____

_____

5. How does what you learned in this American Story change or reinforce your understanding of Native American life? How does it change or reinforce your knowledge of conservation and natural resources?

_____

_____

6. Debate the Issue Form a group with three other classmates. Discuss and make a list of the pros and cons of the construction of the Dakota Access Pipeline (DAPL). After your list is complete, two group members will represent the pro side and the other two group members will represent the con side. Decide who will represent which side and then stage a short debate. Take notes below.

_____

_____

HISTORY NOTEBOOK | UNIT **9** | THROUGH THE LENS, AMERICAN PLACES
New Orleans, Louisiana

The Gulf Coast is home to one of the United States' most resilient cities, New Orleans, Louisiana. What makes the city so strong? Find out why in this American Places lesson. After learning about New Orleans, review the questions below and record your thoughts.

1. **Reading Check** Why is New Orleans considered a resilient city?

_____

_____

_____

2. **Identify Problems and Solutions** What problems did Hurricane Katrina reveal? Which problems have been resolved and how?

_____

_____

_____

_____

3. Why do you think New Orleans culture and character remains so strong despite the economic and social impact of Hurricane Katrina?

_____

_____

_____

_____

4. **Interpret Maps** Use a map in your textbook or a classroom map to locate this American Place. Figure out roughly how far this place is from where you live. How do the geography and topography of this place differ from those where you live?

_____

_____

_____

5. Have you ever visited New Orleans? Write a few sentences about your experience there. If you haven't visited the city, write a few sentences about why you might or might not want to do so.

_____

_____

_____

HISTORY NOTEBOOK | UNIT **9** | **AMERICAN VOICES** **Barack Hussein Obama II, Michelle LaVaughn Robinson Obama**

As the first African-American president, Barack Obama and First Lady Michelle Obama made history. Explore more about their lives in this American Voices lesson.

1. **Reading Check** What events led to Barack Obama's presidency?

_____

_____

_____

2. Do you see Barack Obama as a role model? If so, why? If not why not? Do you see Michelle Obama as a role model? If so, why? If not why not?

_____

_____

_____

_____

3. **Evaluate** How would you describe President Obama's leadership style? Do you think it was effective, and why or why not? What traits do you think a good leader should have?

_____

_____

_____

_____

4. **Identify** What skills and personal qualities do you think a person needs in order to be a powerful orator? What skills and traits do you think a person needs in order to be First Lady or First Gentleman?

_____

_____

_____

5. President Obama had charges directed against him that most people believed to be false. Have you ever had a time when someone falsely accused you of something or said something about you that wasn't true? How did you handle it? Write about that experience below. Remember, this is a space for you to write your thoughts, feelings, and reactions for your own reference.

_____

_____

_____

_____

HISTORY NOTEBOOK | UNIT 9 | NATIONAL GEOGRAPHIC EXPLORER
Tristram Stuart

NATIONAL GEOGRAPHIC
LEARNING

Can you imagine feeding 5,000 people on food scraps? That's just what National Geographic Explorer Tristram Stuart does. He has spent his life reducing food waste, and Feeding the 5,000 is his initiative to feed communities for free using food that would be discarded. This initiative is just one of the many ways Stuart works toward eliminating food waste for good.

1. Reading Check What are some of the reasons one third of food around the world is wasted or thrown out?

_____

_____

2. After reading this lesson, what were you most surprised to learn? What was most interesting to you and why?

_____

_____

_____

3. Describe Study the photograph of the "imperfect" produce. What adjectives would you use to describe the produce? Does it matter what the produce looks like? Why or why not?

_____

_____

_____

4. Ask Questions Imagine you get to interview Tristram Stuart for your school web site or a local newspaper. What are three important questions you want to ask him?

_____

_____

_____

5. Identify Problems and Solutions What Stuart does on a global scale could be applied on a small, local scale—even at school or in your community. What can you do at home, school, or in your community to help reduce food waste? Write up a plan for your project to present to your school or community leaders.

_____

_____

_____

_____

_____

HISTORY NOTEBOOK | UNIT 9
REID ON THE ROAD
The Statue of Liberty

NATIONAL GEOGRAPHIC
L E A R N I N G

Who doesn't like to receive gifts? The greatest gift the United States received is the Statue of Liberty, which was a gift from France. After watching the video about the Statue of Liberty, record your thoughts and reactions below.

1. **Identify** What is the origin of the Statue of Liberty?

_____

_____

2. **Draw Conclusions** How does the video help you understand the origin and purpose of the Statue of Liberty? What does it tell you about the statue's purpose?

_____

_____

_____

3. **Make Inferences** Why might people coming to the United States today still see the Statue of Liberty as a welcoming symbol?

_____

_____

_____

4. **Explore Identity** Do you see the Statue of Liberty as a symbol of the American identity? If so, why? If not, why not, and what building or object do you think symbolizes the American identity?

_____

_____

_____

5. At the base of the statue, a poem is inscribed. Listen to the poem again. What do the words mean to you? What is your initial reaction and how do you feel when you hear the poem?

_____

_____

_____

_____

_____

_____

_____

Name _____

HISTORY NOTEBOOK | **UNIT 9** | **THROUGH THE LENS**
Lynsey Addario

National Geographic photographer and award-winning photojournalist Lynsey Addario's work has taken her all over the world, from Argentina to India to Iraq. After 9/11, she covered the war in Afghanistan as well as women's education issues there. Dedicated to human-rights issues, she continues to capture powerful images in dangerous locations around the world, taking her lens on the front lines of war.

1. **Reading Check** What does National Geographic photographer Lynsey Addario hope to accomplish with her photographs of refugees?

_____

_____

_____

2. **Analyze Language Use** What does Addario mean when she says she is "just a messenger"?

_____

_____

_____

3. **Evaluate** Lynsey Addario notes that you can tell stories with pictures. How could a photo do that? Which do you think is more powerful—a written passage or a photograph about the same thing?

_____

_____

_____

4. **Describe** Study the photographs. How would you describe the mood and emotions conveyed in each photograph? What adjectives would you use? What emotions are evoked for you as the viewer?

_____

_____

_____

5. Each photograph shown tells a story. Pick one photograph and write the story you think it tells. First write it without looking up additional information. Note your initial reactions, details you see, and what you find interesting or moving. Then do additional research to add to the story if necessary.

_____

_____

_____

_____

From the Apple computer to Microsoft software to the Google search engine, technology has made our lives easier. Learn about the leaders and innovators behind the technology in this American Gallery, and answer the questions below.

1. **Evaluate** Which photograph in this American Gallery do you think tells the most about the development of technology in the United States? Explain why you selected the image you chose and what it says about technology.

_____

_____

_____

2. **Visual Literacy** Develop your skills of observation. Pick one of the photographs in the gallery and write three questions you think you should be asking as you look at the image. If you know the answers to your questions, write the answers too.

_____

_____

_____

3. Of the technology leaders featured in this American Gallery, who do you think made the biggest contribution to technology development and why? Conduct online research to find out more about the technology leader you chose and write a short bio about him.

_____

_____

_____

4. **Compare and Contrast** Study the photograph of the Apple I Computer. How is it similar to an Apple computer today? How is it different?

_____

_____

5. **Determine Chronology** What technological advances were created, and how did they develop in the 21st century? Choose one technology, such as the Apple computer or the evolution of social media, and create a time line of key milestones of that technology's development.

_____

_____

6. Who else would you consider a "technology titan" today? What other technological advances have been made in the 21st century? Which one do you think is the most significant and why?

_____

_____

HISTORY NOTEBOOK | **UNIT 9** | **UNIT WRAP-UP**
Challenges of a New Century

NATIONAL GEOGRAPHIC
L E A R N I N G

This unit, Challenges of a New Century, examines recent U.S. history and how the course of American life has changed over the 20th and 21st centuries. Use the questions below to think about what you learned in Unit 9.

A. After Reading Once you've completed Unit 9, revisit the chapters to select the topic that you find most interesting.

1. What is the topic I found most interesting in this unit?

_____

2. How or why does this topic interest me?

_____

3. What are some of the most important take-aways you got from this unit?

_____

_____

4. How does this topic relate to my life, my family, my community, and my identity?

_____

_____

B. U.S. Climate Refugees Race Against Time Review the article and respond to the questions below.

5. What is the subject of the article?

_____

6. What problems is the Biloxi-Chitimacha-Choctaw tribe facing and how are some of them being resolved?

_____

_____

7. How does this article connect with the focus of the unit? Why do you think the editors of this U.S. History program selected this article for this unit?

_____

_____

_____

C. Unit Activities As you prepare for your unit inquiry and the learning framework, record any thoughts, ideas, or lingering questions below.

_____

_____

_____

_____

HISTORY NOTEBOOK UNIT **9**

THROUGH THE LENS
America Through the Decades

NATIONAL GEOGRAPHIC
L E A R N I N G

This Through the Lens features captures iconic photographs from each decade in U.S. history, from the 1900s to the 2010s. Take a moment to study each photograph and then reflect on your thoughts below.

1. Reading Check Can you identify each photograph with the correct decade? Name the decade and identify the significance of each photograph shown here.

_____

_____

_____

_____

_____

_____

2. Evaluate As this feature notes, "a picture is worth a thousand words." What do you learn from the photographs shown that you wouldn't learn from a written description of each one of those moments in history?

_____

_____

_____

_____

_____

3. Describe Which photograph do you think tells the most about its decade? What does it convey? List 5 adjectives that you would use to describe the photo. Compare your list with that of one of your classmates. To what extent do you both see the event in a similar way? How did your impressions vary?

_____

_____

_____

_____

4. Which photograph from this feature is your favorite? Explain why.

_____

_____

_____

_____